Overcoming
Laodicea

Overcoming
Laodicea

BILL KASPER

Contents

Part One

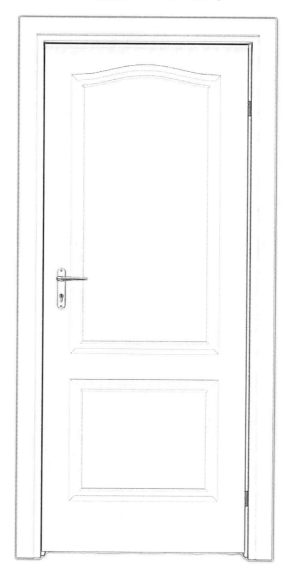

"Behold, I stand at the door and knock.
If anyone hears my voice and opens the door, I will come in to him
and eat with him, and he with me."
– *Revelation 3:20*

1

A Very Laodicean Problem

The wind blew, tugging at his hair. The humid, salty air filled his nostrils. Everywhere he looked from his lookout point was water. John was on the island of Patmos. He was not there on vacation. He was there because of the Gospel; he was there because of Jesus. Specifically, he was there because he would not keep quiet about Jesus. Obviously, not everyone enjoyed his passion for Jesus—he *was* on a *prison* island. It is likely that some thought his passion for Jesus was a danger to society. Little did they know, whoever they were, that imprisoning John on a remote island would not be enough to stop his influence—God was not finished using him. No, Jesus had something greater in mind.

One day, while John was worshipping, he was taken into vision. What unfolded before him would greatly impact mankind. The first scene John experienced was of seven golden lamp stands and a man standing in the middle of them. The one standing before him looked familiar, one like the son of man, and yet different—more magnificent and triumphant. Then it hit him: he was standing before Jesus, *his* Jesus. How his heart must have leapt! He had been imprisoned on that island because of his love for Jesus. The worship session came to a climax as he fell at Jesus' feet. Being in the presence of Jesus again filled him with awe, wonder, and fear. But Jesus touched his shoulder and encouraged him, "Fear not, I am the first and the last, and the living one. I died, and behold I am alive forevermore, and I have the keys of Death and Hades" (Revelation 1:17, 18).

John was then instructed to write down everything he would hear and see, both things that were happening in his day and the things that would happen later. He obeyed. The result of his writings comes to us as the book of Revelation. You may have heard of it; you may even be familiar with it. To many, it is a scary and confusing book—mainly due to the symbolic nature of the book as well as its dark portrait of things to come. According to John, though, it was not merely a book about the future—not just a revelation of last-day events—it is the revelation of Jesus Christ (Revelation 1:1). You see, for John everything was about Jesus. To each of the disciples in John's day, Jesus was everything. Sadly, this is no longer true among professed Christians. Many things have taken Jesus' place as first priority in our lives. Only when modern Christians share the disciples' passion for Jesus will we truly be a remnant of the early church. Jesus was everything to the early church, but things changed.

John was shown many things in his visions. He saw beasts and plagues and battles—each scary in their own way. But the scariest scenes must have been the changes he would see in the followers of Christ. These changes are first revealed in the letters to the Seven Churches (Revelation 2 and 3). Whether you view these letters to be a timeline description of Christianity or a general description of Christianity in any age,[1] you cannot miss the changes they describe. Although these letters reveal people who remain faithful to Jesus, they also show an increasingly compromised church that is spiritually lacking. One letter, specifically, reveals a serious spiritual problem that would plague Christianity: the letter to the church in Laodicea.

Laodicea's letter stands out among the others for an unfortunate reason: in the letter, Jesus has nothing good to say about them. In every other letter, even when there was compromise or error to correct, Jesus said something positive about those who were still faithful in the church. He commended Ephesus for their toil and patience and for not putting up with evil (Revelation 2:2). Even Pergamum, the church that dwelt "where Satan's throne is" and was full of evil, Jesus praised some of them for holding onto His name and not losing faith (Revelation 2:13). Yet, there is not one good thing coming from Laodicea—*nothing* that earns praise from Jesus.

Instead, their condition is graphically described: "I know your works: you are neither cold nor hot. Would that you were either cold or hot! So, because you are lukewarm, and neither hot nor cold, I will spit [lit. vomit] you out of my mouth" (Revelation 3:15, 16). Basically, their "Christianity" made God want to gag. Wow. Of course, when was the last time you were thirsty and felt that a big glass of lukewarm, stagnant pond water would hit the spot? I'm guessing never. Their condition doesn't start off well. Sadly, He wasn't finished. He added, "For you say, I am rich, I have prospered, and I need nothing, not realizing that you are wretched, pitiable, poor, blind and naked" (Revelation 3:17). God is describing His people—members of His church—and they have a problem, a very big problem.

A little history[2] of Laodicea may help shed some light on why God chose this specific city to represent this condition of

Christianity. The ancient city of Laodicea was in Phrygia on the river Lycus. It is said to be named in honor of Laodice, the wife of Antiochus II. Interestingly, Laodicea means "just people," or "a people judged."

The city was also quite wealthy. It was so wealthy that, after it was destroyed in an earthquake around 60 AD, it was able to rebuild (by Marcus Aurelius) without financial help from Rome. This was something very few, if any, other cities could do. It was also famous for its garments made from unique local black wool and for the healing power of eye-salve (known as "Phrygian powder") that was produced at its medical university. In John's day, the city had a reputation for being a banking, medical, and textile center.

It is also note-worthy that the city of Laodicea was known for lacking a permanent supply of good water. Because of this, they had to bring it in from springs in the south (located in the city of Denizle—about six miles away[3]) through a system of stone pipes (another evidence of wealth). However, by the time it reached the city, it was generally lukewarm and tasted bad. Another fascinating fact: the nearby city of Hierapolis was known for healing *hot* springs, and the city of Colossae was recognized for its refreshing *cold* water. Yet, Laodicea, which is in between them, had lukewarm water.

Not much is mentioned in the New Testament about the early Christian church in the city, outside of Revelation, except for a brief statement by Paul in Colossians. According to that passage, the church was possibly meeting in the house of a woman named Nympha (Colossians 4:15), and had received at least one letter from Paul (verse 16).

So, in spite of having fame for riches, eye-salve, and wool, they are rebuked for being poor, blind, and naked. In addition, like the water source of their city, *they* had become stale and lukewarm. This church felt it had everything it needed, and exceedingly so, yet the people were told by God that they were wanting (and exceedingly so).

Again, questions arise as to whether this letter is describing the actual church in Laodicea during John's day, or random churches throughout time, or even Christianity in the last days. While it is possible that it described the original Laodicean church, a brief look at modern, end-time Christianity would reveal that this is, at least, also talking about us today. Think about it: we live in a time when we, as Christians, believe and claim that we have it all. It is a mindset that plagues every denomination. We each think we alone have the full truth. We each think we are the purest group. We may even think we are rich with all our large, fancy buildings and elaborate worship services. Yet, something is definitely missing. There is very little passion for Christ outside the church walls (sometimes there is little passion for Him *inside* the church). Sure, worship services can be filled with a lot of zeal and emotion, but so are sport stadiums and concert halls. Sadly, when not in church, most "Christians" are not easily distinguishable from worldly people anymore. Our churches today do not look or act like the first Christians written about in the book of Acts. It would seem that our "Christianity" is neither hot nor cold, but lukewarm —"having the appearance of godliness, but denying its power" (2 Timothy 3:5)—something that does not please God.

Might God say of us, as He said of Israel in Jeremiah 6:20, "Your burnt offerings are not acceptable, nor your sacrifices pleasing to me"? Or in Isaiah, when He said, "Bring no more vain offerings; incense is an abomination to me. New Moon and Sabbath and the calling of convocations—I cannot endure iniquity and solemn assembly. Your new moons and your appointed feasts my soul hates; they have become a burden to me; I am weary of bearing them" (Isaiah 1:13, 14)? Notice that in both passages God mentions things that He had originally established but called them "yours"—*your* sacrifices and *your* assemblies. They had taken God's instructions to them—His counsels to them—and made them their own. What they were doing no longer bore a resemblance to what God asked them to do. Instead of something meant to worship and glorify God, it became a detestable burden to Him. I can't help but wonder how much of modern Christianity resembles what God asked us to do and how much has become "ours." Could our modern "worship" services, week after week, be only pleasing to us and not pleasing to God?

Like the water source of the city, Laodicean "Christianity" is no longer fresh and real, but has become stale and lukewarm and makes God want to gag. How could His people, the church, get to this point? How could we go from a church filled with the power of the Spirit, taking the Gospel of the Kingdom to the whole world to being a group of people with activities that makes God say, "I can't stand what you're doing"?

Has modern Christianity become lukewarm because we lack money? Look around and you will see that it is not physical money that we lack. Yet, although we feel rich, we are lacking *spiritual* riches. While this is definitely a problem, it is only a *symptom* of the real problem.

Have we become stagnant because we are blind and naked? Again, Jesus is revealing spiritual issues: spiritual blindness and spiritual nakedness, which is very problematic—especially when we *claim* to see well and have everything covered. However, once again, these are merely symptoms of a much deeper, much more detrimental problem.

The root of the problem is found a few verses later: "Those whom I love I reprove and discipline, so be zealous and repent. Behold, I stand at the door and knock. If anyone hears my voice and opens the door, I will come in to him and eat with him, and he with me" (Revelation 3:19, 20).

Did you notice anything wrong with this picture? Did you recognize the real problem with Laodicea? Let me ask you this: why is Jesus knocking on the door? Jesus is knocking because *He's outside.* We often view this scene as a beautiful invitation for the person who doesn't know Jesus. Yet, in reality, this is an invitation for *the church* to open up the door—because Jesus is *outside the church!*

The real problem with Laodicea is that comfort and self-sufficiency has *left Jesus outside.* Somehow, the Cornerstone had been taken from the building; the Head had been disconnected from the body; Christ was removed from *Christ*ianity. With Jesus outside, the inside will rot. If Jesus is not in the church, then it is run by man and is no longer pleasing to God.

Sadly, it is typical for Laodiceans to believe any message of correction from God is for someone else. It is easy to think about another church—one down the road—that fits this description. Definitely not the one *I* go to—definitely not *me.* But it is a very dangerous position to assume God's messages are always for someone else. So, do not think of this as a message for that other church that doesn't believe the same as you. It is for your church. It is not a warning for other so-called Christians who are clearly slipping in their beliefs—it is for you. It is vital for every church, and every church member, to stop their ministries or pause their worship and examine them to see if Jesus inhabits any of it.

If a church's program exists because of months of brain-storming rather than months of prayer, Jesus has been left outside. If a church's worship is based more on what people get out of it than what they bring to offer to God, then Jesus is outside. If your Christian journey is based more on traditions than obedience to God, then Jesus is outside. And if Jesus is outside then you have a Laodicean problem.

It is not surprising then that the solution to the problem is *Jesus.* The cure for spiritual blindness, spiritual nakedness, and spiritual poverty is opening the door for Jesus to come in. The remedy for spiritual stagnation is letting Jesus *inside* again. This calls for a renewing of our relationship—a reigniting of our flame—a revival in our hearts.

Therefore every chapter in this book is aimed at doing just that: experiencing a revival. We will look at the problems plaguing modern Christians—as well as the solutions—and then we will face the knocking at the door. I hope that you will stick with me on this journey. I pray that you will not assume, as Laodiceans habitually do, that you do not need to re-evaluate your walk with Christ. It will be worth it too. Because, "The one who conquers, I will grant him to sit with me on my throne, as I also conquered and sat down with my Father on his throne" (Revelation 3:21).

• • • •

Father, please reveal to me the truth of my relationship with You. Give me the humility to accept my weaknesses and failure so I can be changed and revived. I want to know You again.

---

[1] Those who interpret the letters as a general description of Christianity say that each letter describes all Christian churches in all ages. Thus, a church in any given time could be like Ephesus, Philadelphia, Laodicean or any of the others in nature. This general interpretation suggests that each church examine itself and choose the church they think best describes them. The interpretation that the letters are a timeline description considers the letters as symbolic of the major changes to the Church since John's day. Following this understanding, the letter to Ephesus would be the description of Christians right around the time of John and the following churches would continue through time, until Laodicea, which would describe God's people right before Jesus comes.

[2] David Lang, The Accordance Dictionary of Place Names, (OakTree Software, Inc., 2000), Accordance Electronic ed. ver 2.2.

[3] Chad Brand, Charles Draper, and Archie England, eds. Holman Illustrated Bible Dictionary,(Nashville: Holman Bible Publishers, 2003), Accordance Electronic ed., ver 1.6.

"I know your works: you are neither cold nor hot. Would that you were either cold or hot! So, because you are lukewarm, and neither hot nor cold, I will spit you out of my mouth."
– *Revelation 3:15, 16*

2

Surviving the Zombie Apocalypse

hether you realize it or not, you have been warned that it is coming. Society's concern for it has been revealed in books, movies, and TV shows. Various scenarios have been worked through. Survival guides have been written. Still, some scoff at the idea of a coming horde—passing it off as only make-believe nonsense. However, its arrival is more than just a possibility—it is already here: a Zombie Apocalypse.

You may not want to accept it, but the walking dead are already among us. You may think that you would only find them around a graveyard, but you may also see some hanging around hospitals. You may spot them at your favorite restaurant or grocery store. They've been known to attend schools and go to sporting events and movie theaters. There are even reports of them at churches. They may be reading this book. You may be one of them.

Of course, before you begin to panic, let me clarify. I am not speaking of physical zombies—those do not exist. I'm speaking of *spiritual* zombies. Paul describes them as those "having the appearance of godliness [alive], but denying its power [dead]" (2 Timothy 3:5). These are the "Christian" walking dead. Unfortunately, very few end-time scenarios considered this as a possibility. Imagine the horror and devastation that would occur in the church if it became plagued with such a group. Sadly, this is already an epidemic in many churches today.

It is also the first symptom that is revealed in the church of Laodicea: "I know your works: you are neither cold nor hot. Would that you were either cold or hot! So, because you are lukewarm, and neither hot nor cold, I will spit [lit. vomit] you out of my mouth" (Revelation 3:15, 16). Here is a symptom of a blandness in our spiritual lives that causes God to want to spit, or vomit us out of His mouth—basically, rejecting us with extreme disgust. How horrible would it be to have God feel this way about us!

We learned in the last chapter that Laodicea's true problem is that Jesus is no longer inside (Revelation 3:20). One of the symptoms that will arise when Jesus is no longer in the church—or in our lives—is that we will become lukewarm. Not hot. Not cold. Lukewarm. This is not a struggle with temperature. It is about our attitude, and specifically our attitude toward Christ. As a result, with Jesus outside, Laodiceans can only pretend to be Christians.

Granted, Laodiceans will be the last to acknowledge this. Remember, they are described as claiming and believing that they have everything they need—while in reality they are lacking everything. As a result, their ability to self-diagnose has become impaired. Someone with this symptom may not even realize that they've become lukewarm. You see, it isn't that the Laodiceans hate Christ and have kicked Him out—they don't hate Him, but neither are they passionate about Him. They have slowly grown indifferent towards Him. They may proudly wear a denominational name tag that identifies them as God's, but their lives are lived without regard for God. They can become so self-consumed that they no longer consider if Jesus is *with* them. They appear to look the part, but are actually empty inside.

It reminds me of a summer camp experience in Oklahoma. One of the several jobs I had that summer was helping with night security. My friend and I tried various methods to intimidate the youth who would try to break the evening rules. We eventually tried to use my car. It wasn't a pretty car but it looked very similar to a police car. When I turned on the hazard lights, and turned my brights on and off, it looked even more convincing. Then my friend told me that he had a pair of yellow caution lights that we could stick on the top of the car and plug into the cigarette lighter. When I objected to the yellow color being convincing, he smiled and said, "don't worry, I have blue and red lenses." So, we set it up. You should have seen it. It really looked the part—only at night, of course! For the finishing touch, we used the camp's bullhorn on its siren setting. My friend held it out the window as I drove down the road. We would drive by the cabins with the car all lit up. Talk about intimidation! I'll admit it was pretty fun. We even pulled over a few speeding pastors!

One night we were informed that there were cars out at the entrance of the camp and we needed to check it out. It was a well known fact that drug deals and other bad stuff happened at the entrance among some of the people in the community so we proceeded there cautiously. Naturally, we took my car because if there were cars at the entrance, we could turn on all the lights and scare them away. . . right?

We arrived at the top of the hill overlooking the entrance where we had a good view of everything without getting too close. Sure enough, there was a car. Suddenly, that car started coming up the hill. There was little doubt in my mind that the driver had spotted us. I'll admit that we were scared. We knew something we hoped they didn't: we weren't cops. I slammed the car into reverse and sped backwards toward the camp. I quickly pulled into a small driveway to a shed that was hidden by large shrubs and I turned off the lights—hiding the car, and us, in the shadows. A brilliant new idea came to my mind: when the car passed by, I would turn on the lights while my friend turned on the siren and we would scare them with our "trap."

We were not fast enough though. And it's a good thing too. When the other car came into view, before we had a chance to turn on any lights or the siren, a bright light shone on us. It was the *real* police! Evidently, they got the call too. (Fortunately for us, after telling them why we were there, they let us off easy: we only had to remove all the stuff from my car and promise not to put it on again.)

The point is this: just because we claim to be something does not mean we are that thing. Saying you are a Christian does not make you a Christian any more than saying you are a marshmallow makes you a marshmallow. Although Laodiceans *claim* to belong to Christ, they do not recognize that *Christ isn't even among them.*

It is a problem that has existed far too long among the people of God. There was an outbreak of it in the Old Testament as well. Notice this report given through Isaiah: "this people draw near with their mouth and honor me with their lips, while their hearts are far from me, and their fear of me is a commandment taught by men" (Isaiah 29:13).

They appeared to be praising God, yet they were not even thinking about Him when they did it. Their fear of Him did not come from within, but rather, it was an act taught to them through human rules. In actuality, they had become indifferent to Him. Worship had become just a motion; it was just lip service. It was as David observed, "But they flattered him with their mouths; they lied to him with their tongues. Their heart was not steadfast toward him; they were not faithful to his covenant" (Psalm 78:36, 37). If we sing praises to God and say that we love Him, but do not *really* love Him and do not even *think* about Him, then we are just lying to Him. This is what happens when we become indifferent, or lukewarm, towards God.

We must not think that we are immune from such decay. The tragedy of this spiritual problem is that we can still be deceived into thinking that we are worshipping God even though God isn't in our hearts. Just as in the days of Ezekiel, we still come to church as His people, hear the word of God, but refuse to live what we hear—our hearts are only full of selfishness (Ezekiel 33:31). Does this image reflect the reality of your life? The horrible reality is that we fool ourselves when we think we are all right—just like Laodicea—when, in reality, the whole time we are only becoming increasingly indifferent towards Jesus.

So what does indifference—those spiritually dead—look like? It is graphically described in 2 Timothy:

> But understand this, that in the last days there will come times of difficulty. For people will be lovers of self, lovers of money, proud, arrogant, abusive, disobedient to their parents, ungrateful, unholy, heartless, unappeasable, slanderous, without self-control, brutal, not loving good, treacherous, reckless, swollen with conceit, lovers of pleasure rather than lovers of God,

having the appearance of godliness, but denying its power. (2 Timothy 3:1–5)

This is not a pretty picture. Yet, if we become indifferent towards God, we will no longer listen to His guidance—our hearts become hardened and we no longer care how He feels. Once we no longer care, we will cease to live for Him and will look no different than the rest of the world. Unfortunately, the phrase "lovers of pleasure rather than lovers of God" describes too many Christians today. Even our worship has become an event we attend to "get something out of." Much of it has become programs designed for our pleasure rather than God's pleasure. This happens when we become indifferent toward God. Sure, we may not proclaim to hate God, but we're really not in love with Him either.

You may be wondering how we can survive this impending apocalypse. How can we be cured from being, or avoid becoming, spiritual zombies? Simple: we need Jesus. Jesus had a special ability to polarize people. When He walked this earth, the people whose lives He touched either fell in love with Him or grew to hate Him. After an experience with Jesus, people would leave glorifying Him as the Son of God, or they would see Him as a threat to their way of life. I don't know of a situation where meeting Jesus left anyone indifferent. Therefore, we need to have a new experience with Him. We need Him to give us new life in our hearts again. We need Him to give us a *new* heart. In fact, this needs to become our prayer and our desire: "Create in me a clean heart, O God, and renew a right spirit within me" (Psalm 51:10).

You see, we need to accept the truth that God does not desire mere verbal praises and empty worship. He wants our heart. He always has. As David observed, "For you will not delight in sacrifice, or I would give it; you will not be pleased with a burnt offering. The sacrifices of God are a broken spirit; a broken and contrite heart, O God, you will not despise" (Psalm 51:16, 17). A broken and contrite heart is a heart that has fallen completely in love with Him. But the hearts of those indifferent are selfish; the hearts of those lukewarm are self-serving; the heart of a spiritual zombie is spiritually dead—so we need a new heart!

Praise God, He longs to give us such a heart! Notice what He says,

> I will give you a new heart, and a new spirit I will put within you. And I will remove the heart of stone from your flesh and give you a heart of flesh. And I will put my Spirit within you, and cause you to walk in my statutes and be careful to obey my rules. (Ezekiel 36:26, 27)

God wants to remove our old, hardened, dead hearts of stone and give us new, vibrant, living hearts of flesh. The original Giver of Life can once again give us new life. The One who has the power to raise the dead can revive the dry bones of spiritual indifference (Ezekiel 37:1–14). It doesn't matter how spiritually dead you are because God can revive you! It will not be a partial stone-heart-ectomy either. God says in Jeremiah 24:7, "I will give them a heart to know that I am the Lord, and they shall be my people and I will be their God, for they shall return to me with their whole heart."

This is what this is all about: returning to God with your *whole* heart. God does not want to go halvsies with you; He wants *all* of you. This is why, when finding us lukewarm, He is disgusted. He'd rather we be all His or not His at all—not some pretend Christian. So, He presents us with a choice: "choose this day whom you will serve" (Joshua 24:15). No longer holding on to this in-between stuff—no longer spiritual zombies. We cannot continue to live with indifference. We must not be satisfied with being lukewarm. We have to pick a side—hot or cold—and *live it.*

You see, you are either God's child or you are not. If you are going to claim that you are God's child, then "love the Lord your God with *all* your heart and with *all* your soul and with *all* your might" (Deuteronomy 6:5, emphasis mine). That's a lot of "alls." This is because God never says, "love me with *part* of your heart," or "*most* of your strength." He desires *all* of you—all of your emotions, all of your thoughts, all of your effort. He wants you to love Him with all that you are. In other words, if you are going to say that you follow God, then follow Him with everything you are; put all of yourself into the relationship. On the other hand, if you do not want to follow God—obeying His commands and serving Him—then why pretend? Why call yourself His follower in the first place?

I believe that you do want to be God's or you wouldn't be reading a book like this. Yes, it is scary. Yes, it sounds like a lot of work. But remember, the heart that will love Him and desire to do His will is the heart *He gives you.* Your heart, which may be filled with fear and a lack of desire for God, can be replaced.

Maybe you have already been infected with this indifference or selfishness and forgot about the Savior you first fell in love with. Maybe you need a heart transplant. Friend, God is able and willing to give you a new heart, one that loves Him completely. If you will trust Him, He can give you new life in Him, curing any spiritual lukewarmness. You can trust Him. I urge you to give Him your heart—your whole heart—right now.

•　•　•　•

Father, create in me a clean heart and renew a right spirit within me. Give me a heart of flesh that desires to know you and obey you. Cure me from indifference and fill me with a renewed passion for you.

> "For you know the grace of our Lord Jesus Christ,
> that though he was rich, yet for your sake he became poor,
> so that you by his poverty might become rich."
> – *2 Corinthians 8:9*

3

Good News for the Poor and Pitiful

A lot of wealth was tied into the grand passenger liner with the equally grand name: the Titanic. It was intended to be the grandest luxury ship the world had ever known. All of life's comforts, the best of the best, were offered and enjoyed. Some of what was experienced on board this massive passenger liner included beautiful rooms, the famous grand staircase, and some of the most modern exercise equipment available at the time. Third class tickets for the trip to New York went for about $40, or $900 today. A First Class ticket would have gone for $2500, or $57,000 today, with the most expensive First Class suites costing around $4300 (which is a lot even now) or about $103,000 today!

The ship's passengers on its maiden voyage to New York also included some of the wealthiest people in the world, including Colonel John Jacob Astor IV, who was the wealthiest passenger aboard the ship and one of the richest men in the world (a multimillionaire whose estimated worth was $100 million in 1912—which would be about $2.4 billion today). In fact, there were approximately $500 million ($12 billion today) of valuables on board when the "unsinkable" Titanic hit an iceberg late on April 14, 1912.

Unfortunately, not a penny of all that wealth could keep the ship from sinking. The crew felt such confidence in the ship that they were not prepared should it sink. To add insult to injury, they didn't have enough lifeboats on board (although, strangely, they had more than was required by the laws of the day), and when they actually began to use them, they didn't fill them to capacity—the first lifeboat to be launched carried only 27 people even though it was rated to hold 65. Some lifeboats had as few as thirteen people in them. That night, more than 1500 passengers and crew (of the 2,224 total on board) faced a very glaring fact: their worldly securities were worthless to save them.

Even still today, it is an easy temptation to lean toward trusting in our personal power, position, and wealth to "get us through." It is common to see people, in every walk of life, trying to find security by obtaining some personal possession. Whether it is a little more money in a paycheck, a little higher position of authority, a bigger house, nicer car, or better brand-named anything, many have come to believe that by gaining that one more *thing*, they'll feel safe-*er*. Yet, rarely is that "one more thing" enough.

This, sadly, is also a common impulse among Christians. Many who proclaim to be following Christ actually place more trust in the "almighty" dollar. This is because we Christians have a stubborn problem of looking to the world's dictionary for the meaning of spiritual things. As a result, we often come to believe that we are successful because we are the highest-ranking person in the room (or the smartest, the richest, or the most beautiful). We may start to think that we are safe and secure because we own the right brands or paid the most money. Don't get me wrong. It is not a sin to own nice things. Having big goals or nice possessions isn't wrong, but we can become distracted by them—becoming satisfied with *our* life, abilities, and strengths—and lose all desire for God's plans and the life He wants to give us. So we must be extremely careful. Jesus said, "For where your treasure is, there your heart will be also" (Matthew 6:21). You see, ultimately, our focus will change: if we no longer look to God for things of value, we will look to the world instead.

No wonder God rebukes Laodicea. This group clearly has their definitions mixed up. They proudly proclaim, and truly believe, that they are rich, while according to God's lexicon they are "wretched, pitiable, poor, blind and naked" (Revelation 3:17). They believe they have everything they need. They are *comfortable*—they feel *secure*—yet, something vital is missing.

They are like the rich man in Jesus' parable (Luke 12:15–21) who had a huge crop and didn't know where to put it all. So he decided to tear down his older barns and build nice, big new ones. He made them so large that he could store all of his crop and anything else he needed. He would be set for life. Afterwards, he would be able to relax—he would have plenty to live on for a long time. He had nothing to worry about, only to "eat, drink and be merry." Little did he know though, that night he would die and all his riches would do him no good (nor would they do anyone else any good). Jesus concludes by saying, "So is the one who lays up treasure for himself and is not rich toward God" (Luke 12:21).

Like Laodicea, though he may have been rich by the world's definition, he was not rich towards God. In fact, in the parable, God calls the man a fool. It is not a good thing if God calls you a fool. If anything, this is a great example of how *not* to live.

You see, this rich man's, and Laodicea's, poverty is not the kind the world would normally recognize. It is not a poverty of finances or position, but rather a poverty that is described in Jeremiah 5:4 as follows: "Then I said, 'These are only the poor; they have no sense; for they do not know the way of the Lord, the justice of their God.'" They were not poor because of a lack of money. They were poor because they did not know God. Thus, it is when we do not know God that we become poor (and pitiful) in Heaven's view. We have already learned that Laodicea's real problem was that Jesus was outside. With Him outside, how could they know Him? Consequently, the root-problem causes another symptom: *spiritual* poverty.

Strangely, it is when we are spiritually poor that we come to imagine we are rich. Observe the claims of those who think they are rich: "Ephraim has said, 'Ah, but I am rich; I have found wealth for myself; in all my labors they cannot find in me iniquity or sin'" (Hosea 12:8). This is in great contrast from verse one of that chapter, where God rebuked Ephraim (one of the twelve tribes of Israel) for their many sins. It is scary to think that this symptom of spiritual poverty is revealed in a deceiving perception of spiritual achievement. Of course, it is when we do not know God that we tend to assume we are doing better than we really are. We view ourselves as rich because we have done a few things right (Temper mostly in control? *Check*), or we suppose that if we pretend to be religiously rich long enough, we'll actually become spiritually rich. Eventually, we learn to trust more in the abundance of our perceived "riches"—spiritual or worldly—than we do in God (Psalms 52:7).

This attitude is contrasted in the church of Sardis, who believed they were poor, but of whom God said were spiritually rich (Revelation 2:9); or in Paul—the great missionary, church planter, and New Testament writer—who claimed to be the chief of all sinners (1 Timothy 1:15). The closer they were to God, the more they became aware of the truth that they were *still spiritually lacking.*

So, how rich are *you*? Maybe you have become poor and have not realized it until now—a Laodicean would be the last to recognize or admit it. But if you'll own up to your poverty, you can take heart in the promise of these words about the Messiah: "The Spirit of the Lord God is upon me, because the Lord has anointed me to bring good news to the poor" (Isaiah 61:1). Yes, there is good news! Jesus has the remedy for this symptom: "I counsel you to buy from me gold refined by fire, so that you may be rich" (Revelation 3:18).

First, Jesus says to buy *from Him*. The world does not sell what you need to become spiritually rich. Nor can the church fabricate this heavenly purified gold. Only Jesus can provide it for you. Now, you may wonder, how can Jesus expect us to buy something when He's already told us we have nothing? Jesus knows we are poor, yet counsels us to purchase from Him. Seems contradictory. In Isaiah 55:1, God similarly offered this: "Come, everyone who thirst, come to the waters; and he who has no money, come, buy and eat! Come, buy wine and milk *without money and without price*" (emphasis mine). This is the upside-down logic of heaven—the ability to buy without cost. In other words, buying from God is simply accepting and receiving what He is offering. How is this backward accounting possible? This is what Paul says: "For you know the grace of our Lord Jesus Christ, that though he was rich, yet for your sake he became poor, so that you by his poverty might become rich" (2 Corinthians 8:9). Jesus is the only one able to make you truly rich. He can because He became poor (helpless and pitiful) for us and was victorious. As a result, we can also overcome this spiritual poverty. So if we want to receive true riches, we must come to the only source of true riches: Jesus.

What are the true riches we are to buy from Him? Gold refined in the fire. Since this is a spiritual issue, we can know Jesus isn't speaking of physical gold (He's not trying to get you to invest in gold bullion). To what, then, is He referring? Notice this statement from Peter:

> In this you rejoice, though now for a little while, if necessary, you have been grieved by various trials, so that the tested genuineness of your faith—more precious than gold that perishes though it is tested by fire—may be found to result in praise and glory and honor at the revelation of Jesus Christ. (1 Peter 1:6, 7)

He compares the testing of our faith with the testing of gold in the fire. In fact, he considers tested faith *more precious* than gold—dependence on God was more valuable to him than purified worldly wealth. James 2:5 draws a similar connection: "Listen, my beloved brothers, has not God chosen those who are poor in the world to be rich in faith and heirs of the kingdom, which he has promised to those who love him?" James says that we can become rich in faith, which is what God desires for us.

You might be thinking, but how can we purchase faith? Isn't it freely given? Yes, we are all given a measure of faith (Romans 12:3). But becoming *rich* in faith comes at a price. To become wealthy in your dependence on God, it will cost your dependence in *everything else*. This is a cost because it is very difficult for us—we like to have at least one thing in our lives on which we believe we can depend, outside of God. We have a tendency to rely on anything and everything else first, before we're willing to trust God. We easily depend on health, money, position, and even ourselves (even though all of those things will ultimately let us down). However, in order to fully depend on God we have to let go of our faith in all those other things.

This is why Peter says the genuineness of our faith is *tested*. God explains the desired results of the testing: "And I will put this third into the fire, and refine them as one refines silver, and test them as gold is tested. They will call upon my name, and I will answer them. I will say, 'They are my people'; and they will say, 'The Lord is my God'" (Zechariah 13:9). When gold is tested, it is carefully and repeatedly placed in a fire so its impurities will burn out. Likewise, the fires of life can help purify our faith—removing impurities like selfishness and idolatry—and result in a deeper, trusting relationship with God. Jesus wants for you and me to be rich in faith toward God.

Maybe your faith has been misplaced. Maybe you have faith in your pocketbook—you have done well financially and feel that, when all else fails, your money will get you through. Maybe your faith is in your position in life—as long as you are in control of things you feel secure and confident that everything will be all right. Maybe your faith is in your church or beliefs—if you just follow what they teach and mimic what they do, you feel certain that you'll be safe from condemnation.

Friend, none of those things can save you. All of man's wealth, wisdom, and tradition is worthless towards eternity. You may feel rich—and can even have everything this world offers—but when it comes to eternity, *if you do not have Christ, you have nothing.* As Jesus said, "For what does it profit a man to gain the whole world and forfeit his soul?" (Mark 8:36).

The Bible says that knowing God is what makes a person rich. Do you want to be rich? I mean *truly* rich toward God? If so, then you must first admit to being poor (helpless, worthless, pitiful). Then come to Jesus and receive real gold: purified faith. To overcome this spiritual poverty you must learn to trust Jesus again—to put your faith *fully in Him.* Are you willing to move your dependence from unreliable things to an unfailing God?

• • • •

Father, help me to trust You more. Come into my life and help me grow rich in faith towards You. As I face trials in my life, teach me to run to You first.

"Jesus said, 'For judgment I came into this world, that those who do not see may see, and those who see may become blind.'"
– John 9:39

4

A Cure for the Visually Impaired

*C*harlie Boswell[4] was blinded during World War II when he rescued his friend from a burning tank and the tank exploded. He was a great athlete before his accident and in a testimony to his talent and determination he decided to try a brand new sport, a sport he never imagined playing even with his eyesight . . . golf!

Through determination and a deep love for the game he became the National Blind Golf Champion! He won that honor 13 times (along with three hole-in-ones). One of his heroes was the great golfer Ben Hogan, so it truly was an honor for him to win the Ben Hogan Award in 1958. Upon meeting Mr. Hogan, Charlie was awestruck and stated that he had one wish and it was to play a round of golf with the golfing legend.

Mr. Hogan agreed that having a round together would be an honor for him as well, as he had heard about all of Charlie's accomplishments and truly admired his skills.

"Would you like to play for money, Mr. Hogan?" blurted out Charlie.

"I can't play you for money, it wouldn't be fair!" said Mr. Hogan.

"Aw, come on, Mr. Hogan, $1,000 per hole!"

"I can't, what would people think of me, taking advantage of you and your circumstance," replied the sighted golfer.

"Chicken, Mr. Hogan?"

"Okay," blurted a frustrated Hogan, "but I am going to play my best!"

"I wouldn't expect anything else," said the confident Boswell.

"You're on Mr. Boswell, just name the time and the place!"

A very self-assured Boswell responded, "ten o'clock… tonight!"

Blindness, in a sense, can be a matter of perspective. Put a mixed group of sighted and non-sighted people in the middle of a large cavern at Carlsbad Caverns in New Mexico and turn off all the lights and the whole group is now blinded to their surroundings. Although, interestingly, it would be those who had "sight" who are more likely to panic. It reminds me of an experience I had as a camp counselor during a week of summer camp for the blind. I had threatened to turn off the lights if they did not quiet down near bedtime (since the threat had worked every other week of camp). They just laughed at me. They told me they didn't even know the lights were on!

Many things, like ambition or love, can blind us and many of us have experienced what it means to have a car pull into our "blind spot." Strangest of all, we might even become blinded by our sight.

This is what seems to have happened to the church of Laodicea. They were blinded by their presumed ability to see. They claimed to have sight, yet after Jesus' "eye exam" they were diagnosed with blindness (Revelation 3:17). It is yet another symptom of leaving Jesus outside—becoming visually impaired.

Once again, Laodiceans would be shocked to learn that they have this symptom. In their opinion, they can see perfectly fine. Yet, Christians suffering from the absence of Jesus in their lives are not likely to realize that they are blind.

Of course, if you were trying to test this by looking around the room, you would be missing the concept Jesus is concerned about. As with the other symptoms we have seen, this is a spiritual problem, so it would not be a physical blindness. The Greek word in Revelation 3:17 means being unable to understand, or incapable of comprehending. The idea is that Laodiceans believe they understand spiritual things when they do not. They claim to recognize the truth of God when they cannot. As Paul put it, "In their case the god of this world has blinded the minds of the unbelievers, to keep them from seeing the light of the gospel of the glory of Christ, who is the image of God" (2 Corinthians 4:4). Tragically, this symptom of spiritual blindness specifically affects our ability to see the truth of the gospel.

Of course, if Jesus appeared in a room with us, the truth of our condition would become evident. Jesus once said, "For judgment I came into this world, that those who do not see may see, and those who see may become blind" (John 9:39). Basically, Jesus came to turn everything upside-down. We have a tendency to think we can see better than we actually can. Yet, do we really recognize the things of God as often as we believe? Jesus was explaining that His presence would reveal the reality of our ability to recognize spiritual things. As a result, those who admitted their blindness would receive sight, but those who professed to see would become blind.

In fact, a few of the Pharisees who happened to be standing near Jesus when He made the statement reacted with a typical Laodicean response: "Are we also blind?" According to the Greek, they were expecting the answer to be no. Surely Jesus was not talking about them. They *couldn't* be blind. They were the teachers of the law. They knew the scriptures. They knew more than anyone else and could prove it. Let's hold a seminar! Tragically, only a few of the Pharisees would come to recognize and admit the problem in themselves.

Jesus' response was not what they were hoping to hear: "If you were blind, you would have no guilt [sin]; but now that you say, 'We see,' your guilt [sin] remains" (John 9:41, notes mine). His answer shouldn't have surprised them though. In many places Jesus called them out on their spiritual blindness, their inability to understand basic spiritual concepts (see Matthew 23). In fact, in Matthew 15:14, Jesus said they were "blind guides." They thought they could see because they were mildly successful feeling their way through their spiritual lives (according to their own standards), but they could not even recognize God standing in front of them. If they would only accept their blindness, Jesus could help. But sadly, they refused.

This symptom is persistent and has been seen in mankind for a long time. Notice what God said in Isaiah's day:

Astonish yourselves and be astonished; blind yourselves and be blind! Be drunk, but not with wine; stagger, but not with strong drink! For the Lord has poured out upon you a spirit of deep sleep, and has closed your eyes (the prophets), and covered your heads (the seers). And the vision of all of this has become to you like the words of a book that is sealed. When men give it to one who can read, saying, "Read this," he says, "I cannot, for it is sealed." And when they give the book to one who cannot read, saying, "Read this," he says, "I cannot read." (Isaiah 29:9–12)

God said they would not understand the visions and the things of God. Why?

And the Lord said: "Because this people draw near with their mouth and honor me with their lips, while their hearts are far from me, and their fear of me is a commandment taught by men, therefore, behold, I will again do wonderful things with this people, with wonder upon wonder; and the wisdom of their wise men will perish, the discernment of their discerning men shall be hidden." (Isaiah 29:13, 14)

Does this passage sound familiar? It describes the lukewarm symptom from chapter 2; and notice, it results in visual impairment. Verses 13 and 14 make it clear that when we fake our relationship with God, our wisdom and discernment die out.

You see, the idea of "fake it 'til you make it" doesn't fit in our walk with God. Of course, I'm not sure this concept really works in any area of life. Go to a gym and fake lift heavy weights and let me know if you eventually can. You cannot fake being in shape and eventually be in shape. Life doesn't work that way. This is why regardless of the pleasant appearance of our worship or our supposed knowledge of scripture, if Jesus is not in us we will become spiritually blind.

Here's the truth: if Jesus isn't the source of your truth, you will be spiritually blind. If you go to Google before you go to the Word, you will become spiritually blind. If you go to your favorite Christian author before you go to the Bible, you will become spiritually blind. The Israelites were not supposed to follow Jeremiah—they were to follow the God of Jeremiah. The Pharisees were not supposed be disciples of Moses—they were supposed to be disciples of the God of Moses. Likewise, you should not be following any man or woman, no matter how sincere or spiritual they appear. You are to *follow God.* Do not follow me. Follow my God! He needs to be *your God.* Jesus needs to be your sole source of truth or you are blind.

There is another grave warning in Isaiah that we must read. It shows what will happen if we stubbornly continue to believe we can see on our own.

> And he said, "Go, and say to this people: 'Keep on hearing, but do not understand; keep on seeing, but do not perceive.' Make the heart of this people dull, and their ears heavy, and blind their eyes; lest they see with their eyes, and hear with their ears, and understand with their hearts, and turn and be healed." (Isaiah 6:9, 10)

According to this verse, if we could see, we would turn to Jesus and be healed of all of our ailments. As Jesus said to the Pharisees, if we will admit blindness (accept that we know nothing without God) we can be given sight, but if we will continue to pretend to know it all (stubbornly holding on to our own wisdom and traditions) then our blindness is incurable.

So how can we, as end-time Laodiceans, receive sight if we are blind? Jesus says, "I counsel you to buy from me . . . salve to anoint your eyes, so that you may see" (Revelation 3:18). Once again, He counsels us to buy from Him. This time it is medicine for our eyes—an eye-salve—that needs to be applied.

It is interesting that the Greek word translated "to anoint" is the same word used in the story of the healing of a blind man in John 9. You may have heard the story before: Jesus healed a man who had been blind since birth. His method of healing on this occasion was a bit unorthodox (if the man had not been completely blind, he may not have let Jesus continue!). Jesus spit on the ground and made mud, then "anointed" the man's eyes with the mud. Literally, He *smeared* it on. Jesus smeared His freshly made spit-mud on the man's eyes and then told the man to wash it out. The man did just as Jesus instructed and returned with sight. Call it unorthodox, or even plain gross, but a man born blind could now see. What an amazing miracle!

After the healing, the man was brought before the Pharisees in the synagogue. The healing had occurred on the Sabbath, a big no-no that was against the tradition and the laws of the elders. So, they questioned the man, and his parents, for quite a while (a *much* better way to spend a Sabbath, obviously) hoping to get solid evidence against this Sabbath-breaking, so-called healer. When they were not able to convince the formerly blind man that Jesus was not of God—the man himself claiming, "if this man were not from God, he could do nothing"—the Pharisees, in their fury, cast him out from the synagogue. They didn't just remove him from the premises, but also basically removed him from *membership*. Having been rejected by the spiritual leaders, the man very likely felt that he had just been rejected by God.

But here's where the story really gets good. Jesus heard that the man was cast out and went to find him. It is a beautiful thought that when this man was rejected for standing up for Jesus, Jesus personally came to encourage him. The man did not go looking for Jesus. How could he? He had only heard Jesus' voice—he had not seen Him yet. So, Jesus went looking for him.

When He found the man, Jesus tested the heavenly LASIK recently performed on him by asking if he believed in the Son of Man. "I would if I knew who He was," the man replied. "But I've never seen Him before." I'm sure a smile crept up on Jesus' face as He answered, "You have seen him, and it is he who is speaking to you" (John 9:37). On other occasions when Jesus spoke similar words, the leaders responded by picking up stones to silence Him. This man's reaction was different—it revealed his newfound sight: "I believe." Then, he worshipped Jesus. True spiritual sight will always result in our worship of God. You see, the smearing of the mud not only allowed the man to "see" Jesus but also helped him to *recognize* Him as the Savior.

This is the work of the Messiah (Luke 4:18); it is the healing Jesus wants us to accept from Him. But, once again, we must admit that we need it. We have to confess and truly own up to the fact that we are blind. How can Jesus give sight to those who believe they can already see?

Are you blind? Are you brave enough to admit it? Why would you want to stumble around trying to feel your way around in Christianity thinking you have sight, when Jesus can give you real sight? What other option could be better? Will you come and accept medicine from Jesus and let Him give you sight? Oh, Jesus open our eyes that we may truly see!

• • • •

Father, please open my eyes. I am blind without You.
Anoint my eyes that I may truly see and know You, and fall
at Your feet and worship You.

---

[4] John Kanary, "Blind Ambition," in *A Cup of Chicken Soup for the Soul,* eds., Jack Canfield, Mark Victor Hansen, and Barry Spilchuk, (Deerfield Beach, FL: Health Communications, Inc., 2001) 70, 71.

*"'Come now, let us reason together, says the Lord:
though your sins are like scarlet, they shall be as white as snow;
though they are red like crimson, they shall become like wool.'"*
– Isaiah 1:18

5

Covering for the Shamefully Exposed

Shame is something that virtually everyone on this planet has experienced at least once in his or her lifetime. It is often expressed by casting the eyes downward, lowering the head, blushing, or a slack posture. Some may interpret these as expressions of guilt, but shame is different than guilt. I once heard the difference stated in the following way: guilt is the fact that my actions are wrong; shame is the feeling that I am wrong. Guilt and shame do not always go hand in hand. Basically, while a person may escape guilt over certain actions, the sense of shame is often much harder to escape. A person might completely deny the existence of moral standards, and yet still go through his or her life with a sense that "I'm not right."

The opposite is also true: a person may know what they are doing is wrong, yet go through life with the sense that they are all right (justified). This is why some criminals may admit guilt to a crime yet not feel ashamed. Such individuals actually have a tendency to be proud of their crime. They do not feel they are wrong in doing it (as is often seen in acts of terrorism).

This also occurs with spiritual things. Some people may have a sense that the life they are living isn't right according to the Bible yet seem to easily justify continuing to live in that life. This is an attitude that plagues the Christians of Laodicea. They will quickly dismiss any whisper of inadequacy or reason for shame. They said it themselves—they have everything they need and they are all right. Of course, we have already seen their reality: they are lukewarm in their relationship with God, poor towards God, and blind to their spiritual state. So it is no surprise to learn of another symptom, one that a Laodicean might suspect but is unlikely to acknowledge.

As Jesus turned a mirror on them and revealed the truth, they were exposed: they were not "all right," but were "wretched, pitiable, poor, blind, and *naked*" (Revelation 3:17, emphasis mine). Once more, the result of Christ being outside the church is seen in another symptom: spiritual nakedness.

Using nakedness as an illustration of shame is common throughout Scripture. It is an easy illustration, too, since it is something we normally associate with shame. Many have had the nightmare in which you show up some place and find yourself standing in front of people in your underwear, or naked, and everyone is laughing and you're utterly humiliated. Even if you haven't personally had that dream, the concept is so universal that you're sure to have heard about it.

Nakedness wasn't always associated with shame though. In the very beginning, it says that Adam and Eve "were both naked and were not ashamed" (Genesis 2:25). Some have suggested that they felt no shame because they simply didn't know it was wrong—they were young and didn't know any better. I disagree. I would propose that they felt no shame because it wasn't shameful to be naked. God created them naked and nakedness was not wrong. But then something happened. In chapter three, they disobeyed God, fell into sin, and things changed. In fact, immediately after eating the fruit "the eyes of both were opened, and they knew that they were naked. And they sewed fig leaves together and made themselves loincloths" (Genesis 3:7).

Sin caused them to be ashamed of their nakedness. Shame was the first result of sin. We know they were ashamed because they immediately tried to cover their nakedness (which wasn't a sin in itself) and then, when they heard God walking in the garden, they hid (Genesis 3:8). They didn't just try to hide the evidence of the sin, they tried to hide *themselves*, because along with shame comes fear. When God asked, "Where are you?" Adam answered, "I heard the sound of you in the garden, and *I was afraid*, because I was naked, and I hid myself" (Genesis 3:10, emphasis mine).

Adam's response is interesting. It is almost as if he thought that God didn't already know that he was naked. Or that God shouldn't see him naked (even though God created him that way). Yet, what his reaction really reveals is how quickly sin drives us away from God, and how quickly we try to cover it up.

Think about this for a moment: their initial desire after they sinned was to create a covering for themselves, first with fig leaves—which didn't give them the peace they desired—and finally in the darkness of the trees. They wanted to hide the shame of their sin, yet, in both attempts they were unsuccessful.

Unfortunately, we are still trying to cover our shame of sin in the same ways as humanity's first parents. We still attempt to create our own garments. We work at hiding our shame by the works of our own hands. We strive to cover who we are with what we do. We hope that our accomplishments can ease the pain of shame. Only it doesn't work—and never will. If making fig-leaf garments had worked, Adam and Eve would have been standing in the garden with confidence, but it didn't work. Likewise, our attempts at making fig-leaf garments will leave us still feeling naked. This is natural, though, for "all our righteous acts are like filthy rags" (Isaiah 64:6, NIV)—rags that could never cover our shame. Besides, have you ever felt a fig leaf? They feel like sandpaper! Imagine that: sandpaper underwear. It would be incredibly irritating. This could explain why so many Christians who are trying to cover themselves in their own "good works" are often grumpy and miserable to be around!

Therefore, in our shame we move to the next thing: hide from God. It's as if we believe as a child does: "if I can't see you, you can't see me!" Adam and Eve actually tried hiding from God while in the "Garden of God." No wonder so many people today believe they can come to church and still hide from Christ. We simply pretend that everything is okay. Too many are convinced that if they simply blend in, God will not see them through the trees. This will not work either though, because we are told in Hebrews 4:13 that, "no creature is hidden from his sight, but all are naked and exposed to the eyes of him to whom we must give account." Simply put, you cannot hide from God—God knows where you are and who you really are.

So, what is Jesus' recommendation to Laodicea? "I counsel you to buy from me . . . white garments so that you may clothe yourself and the shame of your nakedness may not be seen" (Revelation 3:18). Notice a trend? Jesus' counsel is to buy our clothes from Him. He offers a garment that is *guaranteed* to cover our shame.

Jesus doesn't provide just any garment either; He offers one that is pure white. This is significant—white is a symbol found throughout the book of Revelation: the 24 elders are clothed in white garments (4:4); the martyrs under the alter are given "white robes" (6:11); the multitude described after the sealing of God's people are dressed in white (7:9); and even the armies of heaven are arrayed in white linen (19:14). Probably the most significant passage though, is Revelation 19:8. It describes the bride of Christ (His church) in this way: "it was granted her to clothe herself with fine linen, bright and pure—for the fine linen is the righteous deeds of the saints."

At first glance, this passage seems to be contradictory. We just read in Isaiah that our righteousness is filthy rags, not bright and clean fine linen. However, Revelation is not describing how the bride arrived dressed, but rather explaining what was *given to her* to wear. In other words, the righteousness of God's holy people is not what they bring to God, but what God gives to them. The white garment is a *gift*. It is the same white garment Jesus offers to Laodicea. This is the garment necessary to totally cover our shame.

This exchange is also illustrated in the story of the fall. As Adam and Eve were leaving the garden, after God pronounced the result of sin in the curse, God made them new garments from an animal (Genesis 3:21). There are two things about these divinely made garments we must not miss.

First, God's covering requires a sacrifice (the original was made from an animal). In the same way, the garments Jesus offers are only possible because of *His* sacrifice. Paul explained it this way:

> Therefore, as one trespass led to condemnation for all men, so one act of righteousness leads to justification and life for all men. For as by the one man's disobedience the many were made sinners, so by the one man's obedience the many will be made righteous. (Romans 5:18, 19)

The righteousness that is white and pure is Christ's—ours is not scrubbed up and cleaned. It is not something we can earn or create ourselves, but His righteousness is "granted" for us to wear. He died for our sins so we could live in *His* righteousness. What a gift!

Second, (and this is something that we do not often think about) in order to accept God's covering for shame, Adam and Eve had to *take off* their fig leaf coverings. They had to stand naked again before God—not hiding it or denying it, but confessing it. Only then could God truly cover their shame. Paul also described this process:

> [You were taught] to put off your old self, which belongs to your former manner of life and is corrupt through deceitful desires, and to be renewed in the spirit of your minds, and to put on the new self, created after the likeness of God in true righteousness and holiness. (Ephesians 4:22–24)

If we wish to be covered in the righteousness of Christ, then we need to take off our righteousness (the works we believe are earning us eternal life). Then, instead of claiming to be all right, we must admit that we are spiritually naked (this is the renewing of our mind). We must become truly naked before God—owning up to the wretchedness that we are. It is only after this change that we are able to put on the new self, pure and clean. Why would we want to refuse such an amazing offer of forgiveness and hope?

A story is told of a Native American and a white man who were deeply moved by the same sermon. That very night, the Native American received Jesus as his Savior, but for days the white man refused to accept Christ. At last he too repented and enjoyed the sweet peace of having his sins forgiven. Later he asked his Native American friend, "Why did it take me so long, while you responded right away?"

"My brother," he replied, "I can best explain it by this little story: At one time a rich prince wished to give each of us a new coat. You shook your head and replied, 'I don't think so; mine looks good enough.' When he made the same offer to me, I looked at my old blanket and said, 'This is good for nothing,' and gratefully accepted the beautiful garment. You wouldn't give up your own righteousness. But knowing I had no goodness of my own, I immediately received the Lord Jesus Christ and His righteousness." The only reason we might refuse Jesus' gift of His white garment is that we think our clothes are good enough.

How about you? Is your garment good enough? Are you still confident in your own righteousness? Why continue to suffer the shame of sin and the useless attempts at covering yourself? God offers you a new garment—His Righteousness—which is so much better than what you have tried to wear. All you have to do is come to Jesus and accept His offer. Isaiah 1:18 says, "'Come now, let us reason together, says the Lord: though your sins are like scarlet, they shall be as white as snow; though they are red like crimson, they shall become like wool.'" Isn't this what you really want? Aren't you tired of the shame? Jesus' offer still stands. Don't wait. Accept His offer right now so He can cover your shame and make you whiter than snow!

• • • •

Father, I am here, naked before you. I am miserable trying to cover myself. Please cover my shame with Your righteousness. Wash me and make me whiter than snow.

"Those whom I love, I reprove and discipline,
so be zealous and repent. Behold, I stand at the door and knock.
If anyone hears my voice and opens the door,
I will come in to him and eat with him, and he with me."
– *Revelation 3:19, 20*

6

Responding to the Knock

I want you to take a moment to think about how many different decisions you had to make just to get ready this morning. What time to get up? Shower or bath or just extra deodorant? What to wear? What to eat? Which mode of transportation? Which route do you take to get to your destination? Do you even go out, or do you just stay home?

Every day we are confronted with many choices. Some of the decisions that we make have very little impact on our lives, such as what and where to eat. Other decisions can significantly change the course of our lives, such as what career we choose, if we decide to get married, or if we choose to have children.

Some choices are easy to make while others are more difficult. Sometimes you might desire to be the one to make the selection, while other times you wish you didn't have to. There are, of course, those who do not like to make decisions regardless of their difficulty. You can ask such people, "Do you have trouble making decisions?" And they'll probably answer, "Yes and no." I find it interesting, though, that even the people who do not wish to make a decision have often already made one anyway. Like when deciding where to eat, they may answer, "Anywhere is fine with me." Yet, when a place is suggested, they answer, "No, I'm not in the mood for that."

Whether we like to make decisions or not, we are faced with many forks in the road during our lifetime—no less when it comes to our relationship with God. A quick survey of scripture would reveal that God frequently brings us to times of decision. It started at the very beginning: which tree do you choose?

Ever since that day, we are faced with the same essence of that question: do we trust God? Throughout the Old and New Testaments, this question has been presented in different ways: "[C]hoose this day whom you will serve" (Joshua 24:15). "Who do you say that I am?" (Luke 9:20). Will you take the wide road or the narrow road (Matthew 7:13, 14)? Or how about this one: Knock, knock (Revelation 3:20)? No, it's not the beginning of a joke, but it is the beginning of a very crucial decision.

Yes, even the end-time Laodiceans face a major fork in the road when choosing whether or not to respond to the knock. Maybe you have been hearing the knock yourself. Jesus hasn't stopped. Listen carefully and you'll hear it again. "You are not hot or cold, but lukewarm"—*knock*. "You are wretched"—*knock*—"pitiful"—*knock*—"poor"—*knock*—"blind"—*knock*—"and naked"—*knock* (Revelation 3:17). Every symptom that we have discovered is just another knock on the door. Another thump reminding us that Someone important is outside. Ultimately, we will have to respond.

Some will become annoyed with the knocking, wondering why Jesus has to keep up this constant reminder that we are incomplete. If He would stop knocking we could get on with our lives in peace and comfort, right? Sadly, these are not the thoughts of worldly people, but of Christians—Christians who have become tired of their Christ. What other reason could keep a true disciple of Christ from running to the door and flinging it open?

But Jesus has not tired of us. Isn't that wonderful? Here's the reason He won't stop knocking: "Those whom I love I rebuke and discipline. So be earnest and repent" (Revelation 3:19, NIV). Jesus starts with a powerful reminder: "Those whom I love." Interestingly, the Greek word for "love" here is not *agape* ("unconditional love") as we might assume, but *philos*. *Philos* is typically understood as "brotherly love," but I learned something new about this word. It is about having love or affection for someone based on association. The love Jesus is speaking of here is a love that grows *from a relationship*. This is affection Jesus has towards us because we have previously spent time with Him. Thus, it is the reason He knocks so much—and why He rebukes and disciplines us. Jesus is knocking, and will keep knocking, because *He loves us*.

Some reject any suggestion of love because of the concept of rebuke and discipline. We perceive it to be harsh and mean—like Zeus on his throne with a lightning bolt waiting to zap us when we do wrong—a punishment based on anger. Yet, Jesus' rebuke and discipline comes from love. As Hebrews 12:6 says, "For the Lord disciplines the one he loves, and he chastises every son whom he receives." As a child, I didn't understand this concept of love-based discipline. My parents would tell me, as they were preparing to give me a spanking, that they were doing it because "they loved me." (And I was "loved" *a lot* as a child. I have been told it's a major reason why I'm tall.) Of course, *I* didn't see it as love. It was painful and embarrassing. However, once I became a parent I realized that, because I love my son and want him to grow to be a good man, there are times I have to discipline him. Likewise, Jesus rebukes us—points out the reality of our lives—because He wants to heal us and save us.

In addition, while we have come to view discipline mainly as punishment, the word's meaning contains the idea of providing instruction and training in doing what is right. Jesus rebuked the disciples many times and disciplined (instructed) them to show them the right way. Jesus' "discipline," as revealed in Revelation 3:18, was counsel to come to Him so He could help us. That's pretty nice discipline.

Because of His love, rebuke, and discipline, Jesus tells us to commit ourselves (be zealous) to turning our lives back to Him (repenting). Being zealous is not about taking your time either. When you are passionate about something, you do not need to be dragged into doing it. Rather, it is something to which you devote as much time as you can and will always find time to do. The thing you are zealous about takes all of your attention. You will drop everything to do it. As we learn in the next verse, Jesus is urging us to drop everything, get up, and *answer the door*: "Behold, I stand at the door and knock. If anyone hears my voice and opens the door . . ." (Revelation 3:20).

"Here I am!" Jesus says. This is the root of the problem. This is the reason our churches, our worship, and our lives are lukewarm. It is the reason for all of our symptoms. The reason for the knocking: Jesus wants to come back *inside*—inside our churches, inside our ministries, and inside our lives. This is why He wants us to be zealous. The sooner He comes in and begins His work of restoration in our lives, the better. He's trying to get our attention. *Behold! Look! Here I am! I'm at the door this very moment, knocking.*

Jesus presents the foundation of the solution for Laodicea: opening the door. This requires action—one that each of us has to perform. How can Jesus come in and give us gold, or eye-salve, or white garments if He is still outside? He's not a member of the Heavenly S.W.A.T team preparing to break down the door; He will not force Himself in. He's also not the UPS guy; He won't just leave the gifts at the door, ring the bell, and leave. *We* have to let Him in if He is going to help. Leaving Him outside in our sickly spiritual state is like calling 911, but not letting the paramedics inside when they arrive. How can Jesus clean and clothe you if you won't let Him in? Jesus wants us to be "like servants waiting for their master to return from a wedding banquet, so that *when he comes and knocks they can immediately open the door for him*" (Luke 12:36, NIV, emphasis mine). Not waiting, but opening the door immediately—as soon as we hear the knock.

Do you hear the knocking?

You may be afraid to respond. Maybe you are afraid that your "house" is a mess. You might think that you have to clean it up before you can answer the door and let Him in, as if letting Jesus see your mess will make Him think less of you. Do not forget that He already knows the state of your "house." In fact, He's told us the state of our "house" while standing *outside*. He knows how messy our lives are—He just said that we are "wretched, pitiable, poor, blind and naked." It doesn't get much more messy than that! Amazingly, He knows this about us and *still* wants to come inside. Of course, this is because He is the only one who can clean us up. He is also the one who loves us. Why would we keep out the One who truly loves us and is the only One who can save us?

Maybe you're afraid of *how* He'll clean. Nothing is worse than having someone "help" you clean your house and they put things in the wrong place! You've become comfortable with things the way they are. Why change? We only feel this way because we forget what Jesus is offering us. We think Jesus is going to come in and mess everything up. So we tighten our grip on our worn-out, broken, pitiful excuse for a life when Jesus wants to give us a brand new, amazing life in Him—a life eternal. He wants to give us gold, and sight, and righteousness. Isn't that better than what you have by yourself?

A great example of a messy life is Zacchaeus (Luke 19:1–10). Though he was rich, he gained his wealth as a traitor and a thief. His own people hated Him. Yet, one day, he heard a knock on his heart's door. *Who could be at the door at this time of my life?* He wondered. He decided to check it out. His curiosity led him up a tree, waiting to see a certain man passing through Jericho. When that man, Jesus, arrived at the tree he heard the knock once more: "Zacchaeus, hurry and come down, for I must stay at your house today" (Luke 19:5).

Jesus knocked and Zacchaeus needed to respond. And he did. "So he hurried and came down and received him joyfully" (Luke 19:6). He didn't waste any time. He jumped down out of the tree—he got off his couch—and joyfully threw open the door. Not long after, Jesus was sitting at *his* table, in *his* house, eating with him. Just as Jesus promises us, if we will open the door, He will come in and eat with us (Revelation 3:20).

You may not think this is a big deal, but it is. Do not miss what happened in Zacchaeus' house as a result of letting Jesus in to eat with him: Zacchaeus had a major change of heart—and a major change of life—after which Jesus announced, "Today salvation has come to this house" (Luke 19:9). You see, Jesus in the house means salvation is in the house. Jesus in your life means salvation is in your life. As John said, "Whoever has the Son has life; whoever does not have the Son of God does not have life" (1 John 5:12).

So Jesus keeps knocking. As long as He's outside He won't quit. We'll keep hearing Him knocking through our symptoms. As a Laodicean Christian, you have come to a fork in the road.

And, as Yogi Berra once said, "When you come to a fork in the road, take it."

You see, friend, sooner or later, you *will* respond. There are only two responses to a knock: answer it or ignore it. Beware though—soon it will be too late to open the door. Not answering the door is making a decision. You will either open the door and ask Jesus in, or you will ignore Him and not answer it. Either way, you will choose. Jesus is knocking . . . and waiting.

What are you waiting for? Be zealous! Nothing else matters at this moment. Drop everything and answer the knock. If it is your desire to open the door, I want to encourage you to get on your knees right now and pray the prayer below.

• • • •

Jesus, I hear the knocking and I am opening the door. I want You in my life. Please come into my heart. Heal me, clean me, and clothe me. Fill my life with your spirit that I may know You again.

"The one who [overcomes],
I will grant him to sit with me on my throne,
as I also conquered and sat down with my Father on his throne."
– Revelation 3:21

7

Beyond Laodicea?

The sound of dishes clanking in the kitchen woke him from his thoughts. The meal had long since finished but he still couldn't believe who was sitting across the table from him: Jesus! Zacchaeus sat staring at the unassuming Teacher—there was something very different about Him. Jesus made him want to be a better person. What had occurred over the last couple of hours was more than just sharing a meal; it had been a life-changing moment. As Zacchaeus learned about the rumored renegade Jesus, he also learned about himself. Specifically, how much he needed such a Savior in his life. And the more he learned about Jesus, the more he wanted to learn. The fact that Jesus even came to eat with him in the first place was amazing. Why would this Man of God give him a second chance when no one else would?

Second chances are not something we usually expect. Life is not like some video game with multiple chances to try to get it right. We cannot just hit "restart" and go back to the beginning of our challenge. Sure, occasionally we are permitted an chance to try again. Typically, though, such circumstances are allowed because we didn't totally mess up the first time. But what of those times we completely fail a relationship or situation?

Add to this our fears of failure (especially failing more than once) and it is easy to understand a hesitancy to respond to God's offer of a second chance. We're not used to such grace. Curiosity, and maybe a little glimmer of hope, may cause us to rise up from the couch and answer the knocking at the door, but *then what?* Can we really just start over with our relationship with God? Is there life beyond a lukewarm, Laodicean lifestyle?

I will make an assumption that if you are still reading this book, it is because you have chosen to open the door to Jesus and have a desire to get to know Him again. This won't mean that you are not anxious about what lies ahead, though, because leaving comfort-zone habits is not part of our Laodicean nature. It is natural to be apprehensive of failing at a new relationship with God. For us to end up living a lukewarm life, with Jesus outside of our "Christianity," it is evident that our previous efforts to maintain a relationship didn't work very well. Thus, if we are going to re-enter into this relationship, we need to do things differently.

Jesus gives us hope, though, that our second chance can be successful. For each of the first six churches, and each of their issues, Jesus encouraged them to conquer. It is no different for Laodiceans. After inviting us to open the door, He says, "the one who conquers"—this means that the issues that plague us *can be overcome.* By heeding His invitation to open the door, we begin the process of overcoming. In fact, victory over our Laodicean attitude is not just a hope—it is a promise!

Of course, our certainty in victory does not stem from our own efforts and abilities: "But thanks be to God, who gives us victory through our Lord Jesus Christ" (1 Corinthians 15:57). If we are honest with ourselves, part of the reason for our failures is that we have tried to gain the victory on our own. We have tried to overcome our lukewarmness using our own efforts. Yet, how could someone who is lukewarm toward God become anything other than that? Stagnant water cannot change itself—it needs an outside force. Likewise, the source of a Laodicean victory is not found from within ourselves, but is found in an outside power: Jesus.

Part of our problem lies in the fact that we forget that there will be difficulties along the way. Once a difficulty presents itself, we assume something must be wrong. Yet, Jesus never said that following Him would be easy. He described discipleship as carrying crosses, turning slapped cheeks, and patiently enduring tribulation. We don't follow Jesus because it is easy. We do it because He is our Savior. We follow because He is the Way, and the Truth, and the Life. Yes, a relationship with Jesus is not without its struggles, but we can have peace during those struggles because Jesus has already "overcome the world" (John 16:33). In fact, Jesus reminds us of this in His letter to Laodicea: "The one who conquers, I will grant him to sit with me on my throne, *as I also conquered* and sat down with my Father on his throne" (Revelation 3:21, emphasis mine).

Jesus has already faced every trial and tribulation He will lead us through, and He was victorious in them all. Knowing He's already made it should give us confidence. It's like watching someone larger than you cross an old, rickety, barely-hanging bridge with boards missing and moss overtaking it. Once you see them make it across without falling through, you should be able to cross the bridge with more confidence. You may still walk cautiously and you would listen carefully if the person told you not to step on that loose board half way across, but you would cross. Normally, knowing that someone else has accomplished a task can create a newfound confidence in your own likelihood of success.

Of course, I realized the illustration above is inadequate, because there are some people who would not be willing to cross such a bridge even after seeing a herd of oversized elephants cross without falling through. Unfortunately, it is easy for us to explain away someone else's success. Just because *they* are able to do it, doesn't mean *I* can do it. Here's the reason for confidence: Jesus was not only victorious, but He will also guide us, step by step, until we are victorious too. As John said, "For everyone who has been born of God overcomes the world. And this is the victory that has overcome the world—our faith. Who is it that overcomes the world except the one who believes that Jesus is the Son of God" (1 John 5:4, 5).

You see, our success in this new relationship with God is not dependent on our strengths or our faithfulness. It is dependent upon our trust in Jesus. We are not spiritually strong or naturally faithful. Our efforts cannot overcome the obstacles the relationship faces, but Jesus has already overcome. It is through His victories that we are given the strength and faithfulness needed. Therefore, it is our dependence on Him that makes a new relationship possible.

No doubt, there will be plenty of outside distractions and obstacles—the same ones that may have taken us off course in the first place—but we do not need to fear them anymore. If you have learned as I have (and I pray you have) that all of our previous efforts on our own were not good enough, then you might be willing to try a different way with me: Jesus' way. You see, when we learn to depend on Him, even for the relationship, nothing is impossible (Philippians 4:13). We don't have to be afraid of the obstacles our enemy will put in our way.

Why? Because "he who is in you is greater than he who is in the world" (1 John 4:4). Remember, Jesus has already overcome the Adversary as well—with His help, you can too.

In addition to this, Jesus loves us and *desires* to have a relationship with us. Throughout Scripture, God called to His people to enter into a covenant that is described in this manner: "I will be your God and you will be my people" (Jeremiah 31:33). This statement reveals a relationship covenant. Why is this important? Since it is already His desire to be in a relationship with you and me, He will want us to succeed and will do everything possible to help us succeed. God promises, "You will seek me and find me, when you seek me with all your heart" (Jeremiah 29:13).

Granted, this passage may be discouraging to some, because "with all your heart" sounds like a lot of work. Yet, realistically, every relationship worth having takes effort. We should not expect a relationship with God to be any different. In addition, we must not forget that God also promised, "I will give them a heart to know that I am the Lord, and they shall be my people and I will be their God, for they shall return to me with their whole heart" (Jeremiah 24:7). This passage is incredible. The very thing that is required of us for this relationship—a heart that desires to know God—will be given to us if we'll accept it. This is a fail-proof offer. In other words, the only way to be unsuccessful in knowing God personally is if we refuse to even try.

You see, we fail at a relationship with God because *we* walk away from it. We do not become lukewarm because of something God does. He is always creating opportunities for us to get to know Him. Sadly, many (maybe even you) have been led to believe, by false teachers, that God can fall out of love with us. But this could not be further from the truth! This is what Paul taught concerning God's love:

Who shall separate us from the love of Christ? Shall tribulation, or distress, or persecution, or famine, or nakedness, or danger, or sword? . . . No, in all these things we are more than conquerors through him that loved us. For I am sure that neither death nor life, nor angels nor rulers, nor things present nor things to come, nor powers, nor height nor depth, nor anything else in all creation, will be able to separate us from the love of God in Christ Jesus our Lord. (Romans 8:35, 37–39)

Friend, God loves you right now (regardless of the current state of your life) and He always will. Even when you reject Him, He still loves you. This is why God so frequently encouraged the Israelites to return to Him. If they returned, He accepted them back fully into a relationship with Him. God promised in Jeremiah 15:19, "If you return, I will restore you and you shall stand before me." This is also why Jesus told the story of the Prodigal Son (Luke 15:11–24). Even if we leave His side—even if we are the ones to forget Him outside the door of our hearts— when we come back to Him there will be celebration and full restoration. It is a second chance. It is grace. No, we are not used to it. Yet, it is ours once we open the door. So, if Jesus wants this relationship to succeed, and is offering us a second chance, what should be our response?

I like the story of Moses. Moses was one who was known to have a strong relationship with God. It did not come without trials and difficulties, though. One day, however, even after several mess-ups, God told Moses that he had found favor in God's sight. Some translations say that God was "pleased" with Him. This could sound like Moses was doing a good enough job to please God (like a child striving to please a parent). However, this favor was not earned. The Hebrew word in this passage means "grace"—or "unmerited favor." In other words, God's favor wasn't a pat on Moses' back saying "well done" for all his good deeds; it was something Moses didn't deserve. God offered him grace.

What was Moses' response to this grace? "Now therefore, if I have found favor [grace] in your sight, please show me now your ways, that I may know you in order to find favor [grace] in your sight" (Exodus 33:13). When Moses learned that he had received grace from God, he wanted to know more about God so he could continue in that grace.

This should be our response to God's grace—to the second chance: "I want to know You more." What kind of God would give a second chance to people who have shunned Him? What kind of God would offer grace to people who run away from Him? He is the kind of God I want to know more! As the Psalmist wrote: "Make me to know your ways, O Lord; teach me your paths. Lead me in your truth and teach me, for you are the God of my salvation; for you I wait all the day long" (Psalm 25:4, 5).

As you open the door and squint into the bright light that is beyond Laodicea, you'll see Jesus standing there with a smile on His face. He can't wait to sit down at your table and teach you about Himself and learn about you. He knows it will change everything. If you'll listen and learn from Him—learn *about* Him—you cannot help but fall in love with Him all over again. Some of it may feel familiar, but it will be different. So you may need to make a few changes.

You may need to change how you read the Bible. Instead of reading with the purpose of getting information, you need to read to *meet God.* You may not understand every passage (who does?) but you can learn what every passage and every story says about the character of God. Understand that the purpose of the Bible is not so you can gain enough knowledge to win at Bible Trivial Pursuit, or worse yet, to be able to beat another person in a scriptural argument. The purpose of the Bible is to introduce you to, and let you experience, your God.

You may need to pray differently as well. No longer can your prayers be memorized statements towards "the Man upstairs." When you pray, let it be a conversation. Don't worry about what words to say. Just talk openly to God. Let Him know your passions, your struggles, your joys, and your sorrows. It doesn't matter if you think He already knows those things. He wants you to share your heart, your emotions—all of who you are—with Him. But do not forget to also listen. I was told when I was younger that I had two ears and one mouth, so I should listen twice as much as I talk. This is good advice for prayers too. You may be uncomfortable being silent in prayer, but how else can you hear when God responds? Take time to listen; learn to be still, so you can know that He is God (Psalm 46:10).

You may also need to change your understanding of the relationship itself. It needs to be a relationship that is based on who Jesus is, not how many items you've checked off on your Christian to-do list. Far too often, we default into thinking that our relationship with God is based on our performance. Yet, Jesus said that many would do great performances—in His name, no less—yet He didn't *know* them (Matthew 7:21–23). Instead, Jesus declares, "this is eternal life, *that they may know you* the only true God, and Jesus Christ whom you sent" (John 17:3, emphasis mine). In both of these verses, the idea of "knowing" is based on experience. Thus, your new relationship with God needs to be based on your *personal experience* with Him if it is to succeed.

Because of this, the second part of this book is devoted to experiencing Jesus again. We will look at stories and passages that reveal the incredible love, mercy, and character of God. It is my prayer that, by the time you finish this book, you will have fallen in love with God anew.

Remember: in Christ, you *are* a conqueror. Hold onto Him, and trust Him. When you do, you will be revived, restored, and redeemed. You can have a real, fulfilling relationship with God. It is His promise to you: "Those who are victorious will inherit all this, and I will be their God and they will be my children" (Revelation 21:7, NIV).

• • • •

Father, give me a new heart so I can know You. Please reveal Yourself to me, that I may experience You and fall in love with You again.

Part Two

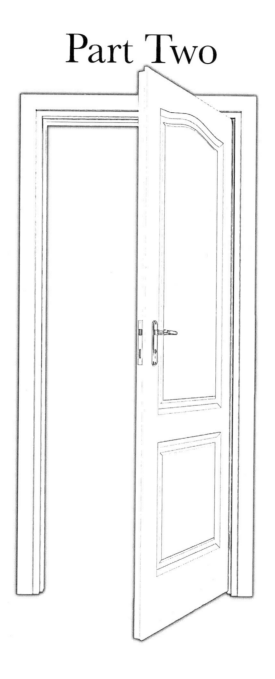

"Jesus Christ is the same yesterday and today and forever."
– *Hebrews 13:8*

The I Am

I heard a story some years ago about a couple returning home from a short trip one evening with their five children. They were quite tired from the day's activities and were becoming stressed from the noise level in the van. To break the tension, they decided to practice a memory verse with their three-year-old daughter. The verse was: "I am the Lord, who heals you" (Exodus 15:26, NIV). However, when their daughter recited it she said, "I am the Lord *that* heals you." They tried to correct her, saying, "*who* heals you," but when they did she shrugged and answered, "I don't know." They kept repeating, "*who* heals you," and she kept answering, "*I don't know*," until, exasperated, they broke down into tears and laughter. Needless to say, after that, the rest of the trip home didn't seem as long.

Although this is a cute story about a child's innocent misunderstanding, it does help illustrate the state of many in the Christian world who claim to have knowledge of the Bible, but

63

are confused when asked, Who? Who heals you? Who saves you? Who guides you? Who protects you? Who is coming soon? Who is Jesus . . . to *you*? The unfortunate response for many: I don't know.

The first goal of a recovering Laodicean is to rediscover the answer to these questions. It should be every Christian's desire to get to know the One whose name we bear. So, after opening the door and sitting at the table with Jesus, we will be re-introduced to the God who wants to be our friend—seeking to remind ourselves who He is.

We'll begin this quest of knowing Christ again, oddly enough, in Exodus 3. The scene opens to a moment in the life of a man named Moses (Exodus 3:1–12). According to the story, he was out in the wilderness tending to his father-in-law's sheep when he came upon a bush on fire. Moses became curious and moved closer because, although the bush was on fire, it did not burn up. As he neared, God called to him by name from the bush. A non-burning bush on fire would already be strange enough, not to mention hearing your name coming from within it. However, this was no ordinary voice. God was speaking. At God's calling, Moses replied, "Here I am." After introducing Himself to Moses, God explained that He had heard the cries of the people of Israel in Egypt and He had come up with a solution: He would have Moses return to Egypt to lead the Israelites out.

This had to be an awkward moment. Think about what Moses had already been through in his life. As a baby, he was hidden in a basket on the Nile to avoid being killed. Though found by Pharaoh's daughter, he was raised by his real mother and learned the history of his people, the Israelites. When he was older, he moved into the palace of the Pharaoh and lived as royalty. Still, he couldn't bear seeing the hard life his people endured. In a moment of weakness and anger, he killed an

Egyptian guard for beating a Hebrew, and then ran—out into the desert—leaving all he knew behind. Once in the desert, he saved a man's daughters from mean shepherds and, as a reward, married one of them.

Moses may have planned to remain out in the wilderness forever. Who could blame him? He had a wife and a son, and was helping his father-in-law with the family's flock of sheep. Egypt was in the past. His present life was in the wilderness. Yet, as he stood in front of a burning bush—in front of the God of Abraham, Isaac, and Jacob—he was told to go back to Egypt. Again, we could understand his hesitancy to leave. He was a shepherd now. He was a family man, a husband, and a father. Besides, the command *was* coming out of a flaming shrub. People would think he was crazy. In a desperate move, he tried making an excuse, but to no avail.

Then, the real question—the heart of the issue—surfaced: "Suppose I go to the Israelites and say to them, 'The God of your fathers has sent me to you,' and they ask me, 'What is his name?' Then what shall I tell them?" (Exodus 3:13). Moses knew his family history. He knew about Abraham, Isaac, and Jacob and he knew about their God. Even his father-in-law, Jethro, was a priest, so Moses most likely learned about his God. But *he* hadn't met God before. In verse six, God even introduced Himself as "the God of *your* fathers." He wasn't Moses' God yet. So Moses asked, "Who are you? Who do I say is sending me? Who are you to the Hebrews?" Moses was really asking the question we all need to ask: Who is asking me to follow and obey? *Who are you to me?*

God's answer: "I am Who I am. This is what you are to say to the Israelites: 'I Am has sent me to you'" (Exodus 3:14). Short, sweet, to the point. "I Am." His name comes from the Hebrew verb "to be." God said, "I exist, I am." It is more than just a name—it is Who He is. It is an important characteristic of God.

David understood this part of God's character. He explains it in Psalm 102.

> In the beginning you laid the foundations of the earth, and the heavens are the work of your hands. They will perish, but you remain; they will all wear out like a garment. Like clothing you will change them and they will be discarded. But *you remain the same*, and your years will never end. (Psalm 102:25–27, emphasis mine)

While everything else may change, God remains the same. It is not just that He has lived forever, but for all that time He remains the same. While everything else may change, God does not. This is a foundational characteristic of God. All other characteristics of God we will learn about build on this one. He says it Himself: "This is what the Lord says—Israel's King and Redeemer, the Lord Almighty: I am the first and I am the last; apart from me there is no God" (Isaiah 44:6). He was here before the beginning and will be here past the end. He exists and always will. No matter what happens, He is.

Moses asked, "Who are You?"

God answered, "I Am."

This is not the only time this answer was given though. It was also offered in response to a similar question many years later. In this situation, Jesus was being confronted by some of the Jewish leadership about His claims (mainly, that whoever obeys His words would not see death—see John 8:51–52). They inquired how He could make such bold claims. Even Abraham died. Who did Jesus think He was? In His response, Jesus mentioned that Abraham rejoiced at the thought of His coming. At this, they marveled—Jesus wasn't even fifty years old yet, so how could He have seen Abraham? "'Very truly I tell you,' Jesus answered, 'before Abraham was born, I am!'" (John 8:58).

Jesus didn't say, "I was." He said, "I am." He was telling those leaders present, and all others who would listen, that He shares this characteristic with His Father. Consider how incredible this claim is: either Jesus is a very bold liar, or He really is who He says He is!

Does it matter if it is true? Absolutely! Hebrews 13:8 says of Him, "Jesus Christ is the same yesterday and today and forever." Like the Father, Jesus doesn't change. Jesus Himself reminds us of this: "'I am the Alpha and the Omega,' says the Lord God, 'who is, and who was, and who is to come, the Almighty'" (Revelation 1:8). In verse 17, He says again, "I am the First and the Last." This is the same language as in Isaiah 44:6. This means that Jesus is the same God who was at creation. The same who walked and talked with Enoch. The same who told Abraham he would soon be a daddy. The same who sat in the fiery furnace with the Hebrew boys. The same who was born in a stable. He was the same who would die for their sins and ours. These are massive claims! Who does He think He is? Jesus *knew* who He *is*.

This is significant: since Jesus never changes, we can have confidence in all that we will learn about Him. The Jesus who walked this earth 2000 years ago is the same Jesus today. He is still our Creator, our Redeemer, our Savior, and our God. He is still the Way, the Truth, and the Life. He was then, is now, and always will be the only way to the Father (John 14:6). He does not change. His love, His mercy, and His grace are all constant. He loved us and died for us while we were still sinners; He still loves us now, and will go on loving us throughout eternity because He is the same yesterday, today, and forever.

Friend, as you begin or renew your quest to know Christ, you need to remember that *He is*—everything you have learned or will learn about Him from Scripture is still true *today*. He is still healing the sick. He is still forgiving sinners. He is still calling disciples. He is still reaching out to catch water-walking failures. Seasons may change, but His mercy will still rain on us. Gas prices may go up, but His grace is still free. Even death and taxes have an end. If there is one thing we can count on, it's Jesus. He will not change.

So, when, like Moses, you ask, "*Who* are You, Lord?" Jesus will answer: I AM.

When the earth was formless and empty,
When Adam breathed his first breath,
When Noah left the ark,
I AM.

When Abraham left his home,
When Isaac laid on the altar,
When Jacob saw the ladder,
I AM.

When Joseph saved the nations,
When the Hebrew children cried out in pain,
To you, Moses…
I AM.

When the walls of Jericho fell,
When Samson toppled the pillars,
When the temple was rebuilt,
I AM.

When I was born in a manger,
When I was crucified on a tree,
When death couldn't contain me,
I AM.

When many died for My name's sake,
As the Gospel is sent to the whole world,
To you, dear reader…
I Am.

As you learn of the past,
As you listen to me now,
As you look into the future,
I Am.

I do not change.
I am the same.
Always and forever,
I Am.

•   •   •   •

Father, may I find peace in the understanding that You do not change. As I learn more of You and Your love for me, let me find strength and confidence in the fact that You are the same yesterday, today, and forever.

9

The Amen

*I*n each one of the seven letters to the churches, Jesus is introduced by different titles or characteristics of Himself. To Ephesus, He is the one "who holds the seven stars in his hand, who walks among the seven golden lamp-stands" (Revelation 2:1). To Smyrna, He is "the first and last, who died and came to life" (Revelation 2:8). He's then introduced to the other churches as "him who has the sharp two-edge sword" (Revelation 2:12), "the Son of God, who has eyes like a flame of fire, and whose feet are like burnished bronze," (Revelation 2:18), "him who has the seven spirits of God and the seven stars" (Revelation 3:1), and "the holy one, the true one, who has the key of David" (Revelation 3:7). These are impressive characteristics. Each one is used to encourage the churches involved in the letter. Each one is meant to remind those churches of the character of the One standing in their midst.

The letter to Laodicea is no different. To the Laodiceans, Jesus is introduced as "the Amen, the faithful and true witness, the beginning of God's creation" (Revelation 3:14). Jesus mentions three characteristics that should encourage us; three attributes that reveal His ability to help us overcome. Since Jesus is introduced to Laodicea with these three traits, it seems best to start our learning of Him with these (we will look at each of these three characteristics in separate chapters).

Jesus reminds the Laodicean church first that He is "the Amen." This is a common phrase heard in churches these days. Normally, it is heard as the traditional conclusion of a prayer or when a congregation agrees with what a speaker is saying (or sometimes it is simply an automated response to a speaker's question, "Amen?"). Very rarely, though, does one hear of it (or even consider it) as a descriptor of God.

To begin our understanding of why this title may be used to introduce Jesus to the Laodicean church, it might help to examine the history of the word itself. The root of the Hebrew word has to do with truth, trusting, and believing. The first usage of the word is found in Genesis 15:6, "And he [Abraham] believed the Lord, and he counted it to him as righteousness." It is similarly used in Isaiah 25:1 when describing God's plans as being faithful and "sure" (or "true").

The first time the word is used as a response, however, is not until Numbers 5:22, in which a woman accused of unfaithfulness was instructed to say "amen, amen" as part of an oath she took before God. Her response of "amen" was an acceptance of the terms of the oath—God's proclamation of a curse— should His marriage fidelity test reveal her to be unfaithful (see Numbers 5:12–22). In a similar circumstance recorded in Deuteronomy 27, as God revealed the curses for other situations where Israel would be discovered unfaithful to Him, the people were directed to respond to God with "amen." The reason for such a response was because "amen" was a term used to agree upon something, meaning, "so let it be." It was often used in the legal sense (such as in covenants). We can see this in the verses leading up to the curses of the same chapter:

> Then Moses and the Levitical priests said to all Israel, "Keep silence and hear, O Israel: this day *you have become the people of the Lord your God.* You shall therefore obey the voice of the Lord your God, keeping his commandments and his statutes, which I command you today." (Deuteronomy 27:9, 10, emphasis mine)

Upon entering this new covenant with God, as He laid out the conditions of the relationship, the people responded, "let it be so." It was a formal acknowledgment of entering into the covenant relationship and accepting its terms—much like the traditional phrase used in weddings: "I do." It was not just the curses to which the people agreed; it was also the response to promises or blessings. Once, Jeremiah was given a message for the people of Israel instructing them to listen to God's voice and obey Him in order that they would continue in their covenant with God and He could confirm His promise to give them "a land flowing with milk and honey." To which Jeremiah responded, "So be it, Lord" (Jeremiah 11:5—translated from the word "amen"). Jeremiah desperately wanted those words to become true. He wanted a restoration of Israel to Canaan. His only response could be, "yes, Lord, let it be so."

Interestingly, while this was the response of the people when God spoke, it was not the response every time man spoke. The only time "amen" was used in response to something man said was when God was being praised or blessed. For example, at the conclusion of a song of David recorded in 1 Chronicles, we read, "Blessed be the Lord, the God of Israel, from everlasting to everlasting!' Then all the people said, 'Amen!' and praised the Lord" (1 Chronicles 16:36, similar to Psalm 106:48). We see this response in Nehemiah as well: "And Ezra blessed the Lord, the great God, and all the people answered, 'Amen, Amen,' lifting up their hands. And they bowed their heads and worshiped the Lord with their faces to the ground" (Nehemiah 8:6). Whenever mankind acknowledged God's greatness and blessed God in their praise, the people responded "Amen" ("yes, let it be so"). Thus, "amen" was not originally used as the conclusion for prayer, but as the culmination of praise.[5]

We see this same usage by the New Testament writers. We find it in Paul's writings: "the Creator, who is blessed forever! Amen" (Romans 1:25, 9:5); "To him be glory forever. Amen" (Romans 11:36, Galatians 1:5; 2 Timothy 4:18); and "To our God and Father be glory forever and ever. Amen" (Philippians 4:20). We find it in Peter's letters: "To him belong glory and dominion forever and ever. Amen" (1 Peter 4:11, see a similar comment in 1 Peter 5:11). We also find it in Jude's letter: "to the only God, our Savior, through Jesus Christ our Lord, be glory, majesty, dominion, and authority, before all time and now and forever. Amen" (Jude 25).

We are even given a glimpse of the phrase used in heaven. In Revelation 7, a beautiful scene unfolds before John. He sees a large multitude of people all dressed in white, praising God for His salvation. Then,

> All the angels were standing around the throne and around the elders and the four living creatures, and they fell on their faces before the throne and worshiped God, saying, "Amen! Blessing and glory and wisdom and thanksgiving and honor and power and might be to our God forever and ever! Amen." (Revelation 7:11, 12)

Upon hearing the praising of God from the multitude, all of heaven breaks forth in praise as well. They heartily agree with humanity—amen! Salvation *does* belong to our God who sits on the throne, and to the Lamb! Then, after adding their own praises of blessings on God, they conclude with "amen!" Whether in heaven or on earth, whenever God is praised, all of creation should proclaim, "Amen! Let it be so!"

There is one other usage of the word "amen," and comes from Jesus. He used it most often when He began a new teaching, usually translated as "truly"—as in "truly I say to you" (Matthew 5:18). It was something He said often when speaking to the people. In fact, the phrase occurs 30 times in Matthew alone. John's account adds two "amens" to the phrase: "truly, truly I say to you" (John 6:53—this phrase is used 20 times in John). Jesus inserted "amen" to the beginning of His teachings to signify that what He was about to say was reliable and true (since He bore witness to them). In these situations, usage of the word brought emphasis to the trustworthiness of His statement. As a matter of fact, Jesus used it in teachings for which He offered no other proof than His own authority. In each instance, Jesus was assuring His listeners that they could trust what He was saying to them.

You may be thinking, this is a fascinating history lesson on the word "amen," but what does it have to do with Jesus? Why would Jesus be *called* "the Amen"?

As I mentioned earlier, these titles were meant to be an encouragement to the people of Laodicea. They would reveal characteristics of Christ. So what does this title say about Him? As we learned, the word "amen" has to do with truth and trustworthiness. Therefore, this name, at its basic level, reminds us that we can trust Jesus—He has the truth.

This is attributed to God in the Old Testament as well. While talking to Moses on the mountain, this scene transpired: "The Lord passed before him and proclaimed, 'The Lord, the Lord, a

God merciful and gracious, slow to anger, and abounding in steadfast love and faithfulness" (Exodus 34:6). Describing Himself, God said that He abounded in faithfulness (from the root of the Hebrew word for Amen). When He promises something, He will always keep His promise. When He says something is truth, it is truth. He is completely trustworthy. Furthermore, in Isaiah, God is called the "God of Truth" (Isaiah 65:16—literally, the God of "Amen"). God has always been the God of Amen; He has always been the source of truth, the foundation of trust, and the utmost in faithfulness.

In the same manner, Jesus is introduced to Laodicea as the One they can trust. He proclaims, "I am the way, and *the truth*, and the life. No one comes to the Father except through me" (John 14:6, emphasis mine). To Laodiceans who are struggling with a major identity crisis and an incorrect perception of what is real, the truth is essential. In fact, the ability to trust Jesus is absolutely necessary to overcome the Laodicean attitude. Jesus is presented as the Amen so that we can have confidence that what Jesus says about us—all of our struggles and spiritual shortcomings—is true. Which also means that everything He recommends as a solution to our problems is also true. Jesus will never manipulate or deceive us; He will only offer us the truth. Knowing this about Jesus' character is meant to bring us confidence if we become skeptical and conviction when we are plagued with doubt.

More than that though, truth is not something Jesus simply obtains, it is part of His character; He didn't just speak the truth, He *is* the truth. This is life changing. In fact, I believe this is the most important reason He is introduced as the Amen. Because this means that Jesus is not only the Amen to us, but also the Amen *for us*. Why would this be more important? Furthermore, how could Jesus be the Amen *for* us? This is what Paul said about Jesus: "For all the promises of God find their Yes in him. That is why it is through him that we utter our Amen to God for his glory" (2 Corinthians 1:20).

There is so much power in this statement. This is a part of the character of Christ that many take for granted. Paul is reminding us that it is through Jesus that every one of the promises and purposes of God are established. Paul also said, "For I tell you that Christ became a servant to the circumcised to show God's truthfulness, in order to confirm the promises given to the patriarchs" (Romans 15:8). God's promises are confirmed and guaranteed through Christ. All of the promises God has made to us can be "yes" because of Jesus. As the Amen, He is the fulfillment of "let it be so." He *is* "let it be so." So, He is God's *Amen*—He is God's *Yes*.

Friend, do not let this slip by. Realize what this means for you and me: Jesus is God's Yes to *every* promise. God's promise to send a Savior and redeem us from sin (Genesis 3:15, Isaiah 53:4–6)—Yes. His promise to never leave us or forsake us (Joshua 1:5, Hebrew 13:5)—Yes. His promise to hear us and deliver us when we call out to Him (Psalm 34:17)—Yes. His promise to forgive our sins and make our lives as white as snow (Isaiah 1:18, 1 John 1:9)—Yes. His promise to return and wipe away every tear, get rid of death, sorrow, and pain, and make all things new (John 14:1–3; Revelation 21:4, 5; 22:20)—Yes. *Place* your *favorite Bible promise here*—Yes.

This is why Jesus is introduced to Laodicea as the Amen—because every promise He makes to them is a Yes in Him. Yes, you can overcome your lukewarm heart. Yes, you can become spiritually rich, regain your spiritual sight, and cover your sinful shame. Yes, if you open the door, He will come in and eat with you. *Yes*, you can have a relationship with Jesus again! When you opened the door and let Jesus in, God's Amen—His "Yes"—came into your life. This means all of those promises are now yes *to you*.

Charles Spurgeon, a famous preacher in the 19th Century, once said,

> If you have Christ, you are saved. Christ is God's Amen. Get Christ, and you have the promises. Get Jesus, and you are like the man who has an estate and is secure of his property because he holds the title deeds. He says, "I have got the estate." "Where is it?"—he shows you the title deeds. "Oh," says another man, "that is not the estate! That is far away in the north of England." "I have it however," says the owner, and he folds up his deeds, ties them round, and puts them away in his chest. "I have possession of the estate." Well, dear friends, we have heaven, we have God Himself, because we have Christ, and Christ is the title deeds of all things.[6]

The One you've opened the door to is the Amen—the Truth of God, the guarantee of all the promises. The One sitting with you at the table of your heart getting to know you is God's Yes. Hold on to Him.

• • • •

Father, thank you for the guarantees you have given me in Jesus. As a result of the promises you have fulfilled in my life, may You be glorified forever and ever, Amen!

---

[5] Some may question this and ask about the ending of the Lord's Prayer in Matthew (Matthew 6:9–13): "For Yours is the kingdom and the power and the glory, forever. Amen." First of all, no other prayers in the Bible, including Jesus' prayer in John 17, conclude with "amen." Second, most of the original Greek manuscripts did not include that ending but, rather, finished at "but deliver us from evil." In fact, Luke's account does not have the "amen" ending at all (Luke 11:2–4). Regardless, even if the phrase was included in Jesus' original prayer, we can see that the word "amen" does not simply conclude the prayer but, once again, comes immediately after praising/blessing God.

[6] Charles Spurgeon, "The Amen," Sermon #679, March 4, 1866.

> "Truly, truly, I say to you, we speak of what we know,
> and bear witness to what we have seen..."
> – *John 3:11*

10

The Faithful Witness

I had the privilege of working at a youth camp during several summers in my college years. For a few of those summers I worked with the camp horses. As a result, I became very comfortable around them and even began to learn their distinct personalities. This came in handy one week.

Every night there was an evening worship, which normally included a skit. Whenever a counselor was in one of those skits, those of us who were not in the skit (or already a counselor) escorted their youth out to the campsite.

I was subbing for a counselor on one such evening, and was leading his youth down the narrow path through the woods to the campsite when I heard a commotion ahead of us. I looked up in time to see those ahead of us jumping off the path like synchronized swimmers, and a frightened mare barreling down the path towards us. My group followed suit, leaping out of the way of the oncoming horse. I knew this horse though. I had worked with her on many occasions. Without thinking (I did that a lot back then), I remained on the path and, as the horse reached me, I leaned away slightly while grabbing the dangling lead rope. Fortunately for me, the horse came to a stop without pulling me over.

After calming the horse and sending it off with another staff, I turned to see several of the youth looking at me. They had never seen anyone do that. They had just witnessed an amazing feat. In their eyes, I had become some sort of hero. Even some of the other staff members who were there congratulated me. Stories of my bravery soon spread down the trail to those who hadn't personally seen the incident. I am not proud to say that it went straight to my head. I started to imagine the legends that would later be told of my deed—how I stopped a raging stampede (stories of legends always have a *little* exaggeration). I knew my popularity with the other camp staff would greatly increase. Many would tell of my valor.

Nevertheless, as the saying goes, pride comes before a fall. So, naturally, my glory was short lived. As the legend of me grew in my mind, I sped my group up the trail, trying to race ahead and pass the others. Just as I was passing a certain female staff member—a large grin plastered on my face—my foot got caught on a root and I fell . . . face-first into the mud.

Have you ever fallen ungracefully, then immediately looked around to see if there were any witnesses? I have. I looked, even though I knew there were witnesses. I had hoped that something else might have miraculously caught their attention and I could keep my fall a secret. No such luck. They all saw me. I learned that day that witnesses come in two forms: positive and negative. Some had witnessed my great act, but more had witnessed my lack of grace. Unfortunately, the "lack of grace" was the story told the rest of the week.

This is to be expected though. It's what witnesses do: they talk about what they have seen. Witnesses are all around us. You and I are regularly witnesses to things. It shouldn't be a surprise that the Bible is also filled with witnesses. In fact, the Bible is simply a collection of mankind's experiences—their witness— of life, God, and God's guidance. Yet, not all of the witnessing in the Bible is positive, especially concerning the experiences of life. Consider the book of Ecclesiastes. It could be summed up with, "been there, done that and it's all worthless." Not a raving review of life. On the other hand, in the conclusion of the book, the author shares his witness of God: "Fear God and keep his commandments, for this is the whole duty of man" (Ecclesiastes 12:13). Quite a different experience.

Of course, a witness is not always verbal. Many times our actions speak louder than our words. For example, consider this story found in the book, *Life of Francis d'Assisi*:

> Francis once invited a young monk to join him on a trip to town to preach. Honored to be given the invitation, the monk readily accepted. All day long he and Francis walked through the streets, byways, and alleys, and even into the suburbs. They rubbed shoulders with hundreds of people. At day's end, the two headed back home. Not even once had Francis addressed a crowd, nor had he talked to anyone about the gospel. Greatly disappointed, his young companion said, "I thought we were going into town to preach."
>
> Francis responded, "My son, we have preached. We were preaching while we were walking. We were seen by many and our behavior was closely watched. It is of no use to walk anywhere to preach unless we preach everywhere as we walk!" (from *Daily Bread*, December 15, 1991)

All of this exposes an inescapable flaw in our testimonies, though. Our account of things is not always faithful. Sometimes we mix up (whether purposely or by accident) the details of what we've seen. At times our memories are faulty. Even the manner in which we deliver our message has the potential of becoming a blemish on our testimony. I find it saddening that while we can have a wonderful message, we can still sabotage it through our method of witnessing. It is like an experience William Sangster had while pastor of the Methodist church in Scarborough. He had an unconventional, passionate member who was mentally deficient and often did the wrong thing. While working as a barber, the member lathered up a customer for a shave, came at him with a poised razor, and asked, "Are you prepared to meet your God?" The frightened customer fled with the lather still on his face![7]

This is why the description of Jesus to the church of Laodicea is so important. He is not just any witness, but is a *faithful and true* witness (Revelation 3:14). The significance of a *faithful* witness is that he will not lie (Proverbs 14:5). So, before any words are spoken to them of their condition, the church of Laodicea is reminded that Jesus' witness will be dependable, trustworthy, and true. His testimony will not be indifferent or biased; neither will it be exaggerated or incomplete. He will only speak of what He knows and bear witness to what He has seen (John 3:11, 31–33). Jesus is a faithful and true witness because there's no flaw in His testimony *or* His delivery. Just as critical to know that the promises Jesus makes are sure, it is vital for Laodiceans to know that everything He says to them is accurate.

The Laodiceans are not the first to hear of this characteristic of Christ. It was previously mentioned at the very beginning of the book of Revelation (Revelation 1:5). In fact, the entire book is the testimony, or witness, of Jesus, not John (Revelation 1:2). Also, towards the end of the book, in a glorious description of

Jesus riding on a white horse leading the armies of heaven as the victorious King of kings, He is called "Faithful and True" (Revelation 19:11).

The notion of Jesus being a faithful and true witness is not exclusive to Revelation either. It was a concept of God taught from the Old Testament as well (see Jeremiah 42:5). In fact, the Children of Israel had been anticipating such a witness. In a prophecy speaking of the coming Messiah, God said, "I have given him as a witness to the people" (Isaiah 55:4). John and the disciples were eyewitnesses of Jesus' fulfillment of this prophecy. They knew well that Jesus was the faithful and true witness.

Jesus verified it Himself when speaking to Pilate during His trial: "You say that I am a king. For this purpose I was born and for this purpose I have come into the world—*to bear witness to the truth*. Everyone who is of the truth listens to my voice" (John 18:37, emphasis mine). He told Pilate, and us, that He came as a witness to the truth—the truth about everything. In His teachings, He shared truth about salvation and heaven, but He also revealed the truth about *us*. His witness about mankind was not meant to be condemning though. It was meant to correct and save us (John 3:17).

We can recognize this in Jesus' message to Laodicea. He isn't being unfair in His account of them, but is faithful and true in pointing out their lukewarm nature and pitiful spiritual state. Yet, He is also faithful and true in revealing a solution to their problem. It is because of this characteristic of Christ that we can know that not only is our sickly spiritual condition true, but so is the cure. A faithful witness does not lie. So, if Jesus says we are lukewarm, poor, blind, and naked, we are. Likewise, if Jesus says we can overcome, we can.

Although it is very important that Jesus' statements about Laodicea are faithful and true, I don't believe they are the most important reason He is introduced that way to the Laodiceans.

Even greater than His witness about us is His witness about God. "You are my witnesses, declares the Lord, and my servant whom I have chosen *that you may know and believe me and understand that I am he*" (Isaiah 43:10, emphasis mine). The main testimony of the Messiah was to be about God, so people would know Him and believe in Him. His testimony of God was meant to help us experience Him. Speaking of Jesus, John said, "No one has ever seen God; the only God, who is at the Father's side, he has made him known" (John 1:18). I find it interesting that the last verb in this passage contains the idea of making something *fully known* by careful explanation or by clear revelation. While creation has always been a witness to God's power and divine nature (see Romans 1:20 and Psalm 19:1), Jesus' testimony of God would help mankind *know Him*.

This is possible because Jesus didn't just talk about God, but lived a life that testified about the character of God. His life was a testament of a claim Jesus made that surprised many in that day: "I and the Father are one" (John 10:30). What an incredible claim! However, this should not be taken to mean that Jesus was saying that they are the same person, but rather that they are "one" as a married couple become "one." It is about unity. At another occasion, Jesus said, "Truly, truly, I say to you, the Son can do nothing of his own accord, but only what he sees the Father doing. For whatever the Father does, that the Son does likewise" (John 5:19). Jesus was saying that He had the same purpose, the same work, the same thoughts, and the same character as the Father.

Other New Testament authors recognized this as well. Paul said Jesus was "the image of the invisible God" (Colossians 1:15; see also 2 Corinthians 4:4). The author of Hebrews wrote, "He is the radiance of the glory of God and *the exact imprint of his nature*, and he upholds the universe by the word of his power" (Hebrews 1:3, emphasis mine).

This concept is not foreign to us. Whenever we experience strong similarities in people, we use statements like "chip off the old block," or "the apple doesn't fall far from the tree." It may be a child who is just like their parent (in looks, behavior, or character), or it may be like a couple that has been married a long time. I have heard it said that the longer two people are married the more alike they become. They begin to talk the same way. They can often finish each other's sentences. Some even start looking the same! So, it is not difficult for us to grasp the idea of Jesus being the image of God.

This is why Jesus declared, "Whoever sees me sees him who sent me" (John 12:45). He was a living witness of His Father. Even though Jesus was open about this, many in the crowds still did not recognize that as they experienced Jesus, through His teachings or His interactions with them, they were also experiencing the Father (John 8:19). How much more, then, would the disciples, who spent intimate time with Jesus and grew to really know Him, get to know the Father! Yet, just before the cross, even they still missed this.

> "If you had known me, you would have known my Father also. From now on you do know him and have seen him." Philip said to him, "Lord, show us the Father, and it is enough for us." Jesus said to him, "Have I been with you so long, and you still do not know me, Philip? Whoever has seen me has seen the Father. How can you say, 'Show us the Father?'" (John 14:7–9)

It is no different for end-time, recovering Laodiceans. As we open the door and get to know Jesus, we also get to know the Father. This is vital. Since the view of God has been increasingly tainted by false reports, we need a faithful witness of His true nature. Sadly, I have heard some say, "I do not like the God of the Old Testament but I like Jesus." Yet, according to Jesus, they are not different. Based on Jesus' living testimony, we learn that God is not a vindictive, judgmental, unforgiving dictator sitting on His throne waiting to destroy us when we make a mistake, but is a loving, merciful, forgiving Father who desires to save us. This is good news! Especially for us prodigal sons and daughters who are returning home.

Jesus is introduced as a Faithful and True Witness because we must understand that He will only testify about the truth. So we can trust His counsel and His example. Yes, the truth is, as Laodiceans, we are in a rough state. We were not likely to realize it if Jesus had not exposed our condition. However, the solution is also powerful. It is possible to be an overcomer! Yet, most of all, the sympathetic Jesus, who knocked on our hearts encouraging a renewed relationship, testified that our heavenly Father desires the same thing!

It is to your benefit to accept the testimony of Jesus—about you, about the solution, and about God. He will not lead you astray or bring you to destruction. No, He will save you. You can trust this because He said so, and He is Faithful and True!

• • • •

Father, thank you for the faithful witness of Jesus. Thank you for revealing the truth of my need for You. Thank you for Jesus' example, which shows me who You really are. Help me to accept and hold onto His testimony.

---

7 Warren W. Wiersbe and Lloyd M. Perry, *Wycliffe Handbook of Preaching & Preachers* (Chicago: Moody Press, 1984), 215.

"In the beginning was the Word, and the Word was with God,
and the Word was God. He was in the beginning with God.
All things were made through him, and without him
was not any thing made that was made."
– *John 1:1–3*

11

The Creator

rapping up the introduction to the church of Laodicea, Jesus is called "the beginning of God's creation" (Revelation 3:14). A misunderstanding of this phrase has caused some to suggest that Jesus was the first one created. While it is true that He is the only begotten Son of God, it doesn't mean that Jesus is a created being. If Jesus had a beginning—if He *was* the first being created—how could He make the claim, "I Am" (John 8:58)? Actually, the Bible suggests a different meaning to this title.

In the introduction to his gospel, John says, "In the beginning was the Word, and the Word was with God, and the Word was God. He was in the beginning with God" (John 1:1, 2). Later, in verse 14, John reveals that "the Word" became flesh and lived among us; he was speaking of Jesus. There was no question in

John's mind that Jesus is God. He didn't think of Jesus having a beginning—Jesus was already with God *at* the beginning. In addition, John says that "all things were made through him, and without him was not anything made that was made" (John 1:3). In other words, Jesus is the origin of—the beginning and active cause of—creation.[8] Therefore, Jesus is also our Creator.

This aspect of the character of Christ is always before us. We are reminded of it quite frequently, even though we may not always recognize it. It is memorialized in the seven-day week. How could the seven-day week be a reminder of our Creator, you ask? Consider this: it is the only measurement of time that does not depend on the movement of any celestial body. A day is measured by the rotation of the earth, a month is measured of the movement of the moon around the earth, and a year is the time it takes the earth to journey around the sun. Yet, no such motion regulates the seven-day week. Nations have even tried alternate week lengths and all of them have failed.

How did we get seven days in a week then? You may already know the story, but let's revisit it again anyway. Genesis 1:1 says, "In the beginning God created the heavens and the earth." According to Genesis, God created everything and He did it in a specific amount of time. He created light, the sky, waters, and land; He created the sun, moon, and stars; He created birds, fish, animals, and humanity—all in six days. These things did not evolve over millions of years, or even thousands of years. It was six literal days.[9] Of course, He *spoke* things into existence— why would He need thousands of years? Then, He capped off the creation week with the seventh day and established a lasting memorial. The seven-day week stands only *because God created it*. If He had finished everything in five days we would have a five-day week. The very fact that the seven-day week cannot be explained scientifically is a strong memorial of God as Creator.

You may be wondering why it would be important to remember this. Why have a memorial for creation, or more specifically, God as Creator? Does it really matter how we believe we were created? Yes it does! Our understanding greatly impacts our view of God.

Unlike what too many (even Christians) are teaching these days, our lives did not happen by some spectacular accident. We did not mysteriously evolve from other species (no, visiting a zoo is *not* a family reunion). God purposely created this earth and everything in it—especially mankind. If we were just accidents—some colossal, Big Bang mistake—then we would have no purpose in being alive, but we were *not* accidents.

Notice what the creation story says about our beginnings: "So God created man in his own image, in the image of God he created him; male and female he created them" (Genesis 1:27). This does not sound like an accident! Have you ever accidentally dropped clay, or Play-doh, and when it hit the floor you noticed an exact replica of yourself in it? It's not even possible. No, it wasn't a mistake—God *intentionally* made us in His image. We are "fearfully and wonderfully made" (Psalm 139:14).

Of course, this isn't meant to give us a greater image of ourselves, but a greater image of God. As incredible as our bodies are, they were created by One immensely greater than us! Our God is awesome and powerful, and we are only images of Him. Everything we have, or that we are, we owe to Him. He is the One "who created the heavens and stretched them out, who spread out the earth and what comes from it, who gives breath to the people on it and spirit to those who walk in it" (Isaiah 42:5). The reason you wake up in the morning and have breath in your lungs is because of God.

This is a very important thing to be reminded of. In fact, God being Creator is the reason all of heaven worships Him. In Revelation, the elders by the throne of God sing out, "Worthy are you, our Lord and God, to receive glory and honor and power, for you created all things, and by your will they existed and were created" (Revelation 4:11). In Nehemiah 9:6, we read, "You are the Lord, you alone. You have made the heaven, the heaven of heavens, with all their host, the earth and all that is on it, the seas and all that is in them; and you preserve all of them; and the host of heaven worships you."

This is also the reason that should cause us to worship Him. Notice what the Psalmist says:

> By the word of the Lord the heavens were made, and by the breath of his mouth all their host. … Let all the earth fear the Lord; let all the inhabitants of the world stand in awe of him! For he spoke, and it came to be; he commanded, and it stood firm. (Psalm 33:6, 8, 9)[10]

We *should* fear and worship the God who can create everything simply by speaking it into existence. We should be in awe of a God with such power. Our worship of God should be based on the fact that He is our Creator, not based on whether or not He happened to bless us during the week. Even the final, end-time message to mankind includes this call: "Fear God and give him glory, because the hour of his judgment has come, and worship him who made heaven and earth, the sea and the springs of water" (Revelation 14:7).

You may be wondering why there is so much emphasis on remembering God as Creator. Understand, friends, that Satan has done much to cause us to forget. It is no coincidence that as people of God were beginning to preach this message of Revelation 14:7 in the early and mid 1800s that a new message emerged. It was during that time—1844 to be precise—that Charles Darwin published his book, *The Origin of Species*. His theory suggested that everything that we see around us was the result of an accidental Big Bang and nature evolving over millions of years. His ideas removed the need for a Creator God. Interestingly, up until that time, every religion of the world (including pagan ones) taught creation by a higher power.

Today, more than ever, there are constant attacks on God as creator. There seems to be more effort given to disprove a creator (even by Christianity), than to remember our Creator. The removal of a creator does more damage than you might think.

You see, if God wasn't creator, and we all just accidentally came to be, then who we are is who we were always meant to be. In fact, according to Darwin's theory, as we evolve we are getting better (even though much of humanity's actions lately seem to say otherwise). Thus, we were not originally made perfect and holy, in the image of God. In other words, by forgetting God as Creator, we forget the truth about ourselves.

Genesis 3 reveals that, though we were created in the image of God, mankind fell from that original glory. According to scripture, who we are today is *not* who we were created to be. When humanity chose to trust in the created rather than the Creator, we fell out of that relationship with God and into rebellion (sin). Ever since that day, sin has been a part of our lives, even from our birth (Psalm 51:5). Romans 3:23 says that we "all have sinned and fall short of the glory of God." Not one of us is free from sin, but we are likely to forget this when we forget about God. And it is to our harm that we forget, because the Bible warns us that the wages of sin is death (Romans 6:23)!

We were created to live forever, but sin has also taken that away. God warned Adam and Eve that if they did not trust Him (and ate of the forbidden tree) they would surely die. Yet this is not a punishment for doing wrong; it is the natural results of sin. Notice what Isaiah 59:1, 2 says: "Behold, the Lord's hand is not shortened, that it cannot save, or his ear dull, that it cannot hear; but your iniquities have made a separation between you and your God, and your sins have hidden his face from you so that he does not hear."

The natural result of sin separates us from God. If God is our source of life and we are separated from that source, then we do not have life. Just as life originated in God, eternal life is only possible through God. Sin, therefore, separates us from the source of eternal life. Understand that Satan wants us to forget God as Creator because, when we do, we will also forget that we are sinners—causing us to reject the Savior.

Satan also wants us to forget that, as Creator, God also has the power to *re-create*. David remembered this. He understood this fact about his Creator and cried out, "Create in me a clean heart, O God, and renew a right spirit within me" (Psalm 51:10). God desires to, and can, change us. 2 Corinthians 5:17 says, "Therefore, if anyone is in Christ, he is a new creation. The old has passed away; behold the new has come." The God who created can recreate. He can change us from who we were to who we were always meant to be. He will give us a new self, "created after the likeness of God in true righteousness and holiness" (Ephesians 4:24).

God hasn't given up on us. He's not a "Watchmaker-God" who started us off in the beginning then left us on our own for the rest of our lives. He's an intentional and personal Creator who wants to, and is able to, restore us. He truly desires to return us back into His image. Isn't that incredible?

Do you see why it is so dangerous to forget God as Creator? When we do, we will not call on God to save us and change us. We will reject putting on "the new self, which is being renewed in knowledge after the image of its creator" (Colossians 3:10).

Here's the beautiful part: "If we confess our sins, he is faithful and just to forgive us our sins and to cleanse us from all unrighteousness" (1 John 1:9). If you will remember your Creator, and admit your need for Him, He will forgive you and cleanse you. This is taking off the old self. It is admitting you need a change. It is admitting you are in need of a recreation.

No, friend, you are not a mistake. You are not a mass of evolved hand-me-down DNA. God *intentionally* created you. He declares, "Before I formed you in the womb I knew you" (Jeremiah 1:5). He did not create you for all of this pain and suffering; He created you for eternal life and joy in Him. Since He is the one who created you, He is also the one who is able to recreate you—to transform you into the person He always meant you to be. So do not forget your Creator! If you'll look, you can see His creative power all around you. Every week, there is a memorial established that can remind you that He made you and can remake you. Return to Him and let Him forgive you, cleanse you, and restore you. He promises that "whoever comes to me I will never cast out" (John 6:37).

•　•　•　•

Father, I recognize that I am only part of Your fallen
creation. Forgive me for my sins. Cleanse me; create in me
a heart that desires to know and follow You. Please restore
Your image in my life.

---

[8] John's statement that "all things were made through him" does not negate the Father's presence at creation. The creation story reveals evidence that they were both active in creation. Consider a statement at the creation of man: "Let *us* make man in *our* image" (Genesis 1:26, emphasis mine). Who was God speaking to? It wasn't the angels, because we are not created in their image, but in God's (Genesis 1:27). What is revealed here is a partnership in creation. *Both* the Father and the Son were present and active in creation.

[9] Some argue that each creation day was actually one thousand years. This idea comes from a misreading of 2 Peter 3:8, which says, "With the Lord one day is as a thousand years, and a thousand years as one day." This passage is not a prophetic key—nor is the Genesis account a prophetic account. In addition, Peter's comment is a comparison: With God a day is *as* [or like] a thousand years. He also said a thousand years is as [or like] a day. Furthermore, each "day" in the creation story was composed of only one evening and morning— or one 24-hour period. Therefore, grammatically, the only way we can take the creation account is that it took six *literal* days.

[10] See also Genesis 1:3, Hebrews 11:3, and Psalm 149:5, 6.

*"And the Word became flesh and dwelt among us, and we have
seen his glory, glory as of the only Son from the Father,
full of grace and truth."*
– John 1:14

The Son

When Jesus walked on this earth, He made many bold claims. He made claims about the Law, about life, about Heaven, and even about Himself. Of all the controversial claims He made, two of the claims about Himself seem to be contradictory. On the one hand, He claimed to be the Son of Man—like us in every way; on the other hand, He claimed to be the Son of God—like the Father in every way. How can this be? How could someone be *both* God and man? It is natural, though, for us to questions such a claim because it is not a normal claim. As a result, three different views developed regarding the person of Jesus.

The first view suggests that Jesus was completely human—a mere man, nothing more. This view believes that He was just another wise man, a moral teacher, or even a prophet, but in no way divine.

The second view believes that Jesus was completely God—not one trace of humanity in Him. It suggests that when He was here on earth, He had all the same powers and abilities as when He was in Heaven. Therefore, this view claims that He never actually "became" flesh; He only looked like He did.

Finally, the third view states that Jesus was a perfect combination of God and Man. That He was both completely God and completely man the whole time. He truly became flesh and yet continued to be the same God that created the world.

Again, some may wonder why this is even important. Does it really matter? It sure does! If we want to know more about God, it matters that we learn the truth. Plus, this is a claim made *by Jesus*. And everyone who comes in contact with Jesus is faced with the question of these claims. John Chrysostom (c.347–407), a fourth century preacher and the Archbishop of Constantinople, described this dilemma:

> I do not think of Christ as God alone, or man alone, but both together. For I know He was hungry, and I know that with five loves He fed five thousand. I know He was thirsty, and I know that He turned the water into wine. I know he was carried in a ship, and I know that He walked on the sea. I know that He died, and I know that He raised the dead. I know that He was set before Pilate, and I know that He sits with the Father on His throne. I know that He was worshipped by angels, and I know that He was rejected by the Jews. And truly some of these I ascribe to the human, and others to the divine nature. For by reason of this He is said to have been both God and man.

You see, if Jesus is telling the truth, then *both* have to be true. So, can Jesus be both God and Man? Let's see what the Bible says.

First, we'll look at what God's Word says about Christ's divinity. An amazing description of Jesus is found in the first chapter of the Gospel of John:

> In the beginning was the Word, and the Word was with God, and the Word was God. He was in the beginning with God. All things were made through him, and without him was not anything made that was made . . . And the Word became flesh and dwelt among us, and we have seen his glory, glory as of the only Son from the Father, full of grace and truth . . . grace and truth came through Jesus Christ. (John 1:1–3, 14, 17)

John is using the term "Word" to describe Jesus. The One who was in the beginning with God, and was God. The One through whom all things were created. There is no doubt that John saw Jesus as divine. But these were not only John's thoughts. We read similar sentiments from the author of Hebrews, in which he calls Jesus God's Son and also speaks of creation occurring through Him (Hebrews 1:1, 2). The author of Hebrews reminds us of what God said of Jesus in the Old Testament as well:

> But of the Son he says, "Your throne, *O God*, is forever and ever, the scepter of uprightness is the scepter of your kingdom. You have loved righteousness and hated wickedness; therefore God, your God, has anointed you with the oil of gladness beyond your companions." (Hebrews 1:8, 9, emphasis mine)

We will hear this language coming from the writings of Paul as well. In Titus 2:13, he says that we are "waiting for our blessed hope, the appearing of the glory of our great God and Savior Jesus Christ." And again in Romans 9:5, Paul says that Christ is

"God over all." It should not be a surprise that Jesus' disciples experienced Him in this manner. This was foretold in the prophecies of the Messiah: "For to us a child is born, to us a son is given; and the government shall be upon his shoulder, and his name shall be called Wonderful Counselor, Mighty God, Everlasting Father, Prince of Peace" (Isaiah 9:6).

The Bible says that Jesus was present from the beginning, He created the universe, and He would be worshipped. He would be called Mighty God and Everlasting Father! Every characteristic of God is given to Jesus. He performed many miracles. He cast out demons. He healed the sick. He forgave sins—something *only God* can do—because He is God.

The centurion knew it when Jesus was crucified on the cross (Matthew 27:54). The demons knew it when Christ arrived to cast them out (Mark 5:7). Satan knew it when he tempted Him in the wilderness (Matthew 4:3, 6). John the Baptist knew it when the Lamb of God came to be baptized (John 1:34). God announced it to the world when His Beloved came up out of the water by saying, "This is my son, whom I love; with Him I am well pleased" (Matthew 3:17). The Bible makes it plain: Jesus is the Son of Heaven. He is the Son of God. He is God.

What about Christ's Humanity? He is God, but is He also man? Remember what we read in John 1:14? "And the Word *became flesh* and dwelt among us" (emphasis mine). In order to *become* flesh He would have had to be born—He would have entered this world as an infant. Once again, we find that this would be foretold as well: "Therefore the Lord himself will give you a sign. Behold the virgin shall conceive and bear a son, and shall call his name Immanuel" (Isaiah 7:14). He would be called Immanuel or "God with us." The Son of God *with us*. Paul tells us in Galatians 4:4 that "when the fullness of time had come, God sent forth his Son, born of a woman, born under the law." And this baby grew in wisdom and in stature (Luke 2:52).

Not only was He born like we are, and grew up like we do, but as Paul said in Galatians, He was also born under the same rules as we are. He didn't get a break for being "the Son." He was under the same Laws of God and the same laws of nature. He had the same fears and hopes that we have. He experienced the same ups and downs we experience. He felt hunger pains (Matthew 4:2) and the grief of a friend's death (John 11:35). He was tempted with power and greed and doubt (Matthew 4:1–11) —yet, without giving in to the temptation. Jesus became thirsty (John 19:28); He became sleepy (Matthew 8:24). He laughed and cried. He was bruised when He was hit. He bled when His skin was pierced. He died when He was murdered on the cross.

Jesus is every bit as human as we are. That is why He often called Himself the Son of Man. In Hebrews it says that He is not ashamed to call us brothers and sisters (Hebrews 2:11). He is proud of His humanity. The author of Hebrews explains how important His humanity is to Him—and to us.

> Since therefore the children share in flesh and blood, he himself likewise partook of the same things, that through death might destroy the one who has the power of death, that is, the devil, and deliver all those who through fear of death were subject to lifelong slavery. For surely it is not angels that he helps, but he helps the offspring of Abraham. Therefore he had to be made like his brothers in every respect, so that he might become a merciful and faithful high priest in the service of God, to make propitiation for the sins of the people. For because he himself has suffered when tempted, he is able to help those who are being tempted. (Hebrews 2:14–18).

Jesus' humanity was important so He could completely understand what we go through. He can truly say, "I know what you're going through because I have already been where you are and I know what it takes to succeed." He knows what you have been through, what you are going through now, and what you will go through later. Because of this, He can then intercede for you and help you in ways you can't even imagine.

However, some still say, "sure, Jesus was tempted with *some* of the same things we are, but He was never tempted with what *I'm* tempted with, so He really doesn't understand me." But Jesus does understand. "For we do not have a high priest who is unable to sympathize with our weaknesses, but one who in every respect has been tempted as we are, yet without sin" (Hebrews 4:15). The Bible may not list every temptation that Jesus endured, but it does say that He was temped *in every way* that we are. That is what makes Him sympathetic to us. He knows because He lived it. Again the Bible is clear: Jesus is the Son of Earth. He is the Son of Man. He is man.

Why is this important? C.S. Lewis summed it up this way:

> A man who was merely a man and said the sort of things Jesus said would not be a great moral teacher. He would either be a lunatic—on a level with the man who says he is a poached egg—or else he would be the Devil of Hell. You must make your choice. Either this man was, and is, the Son of God; or else a madman or something worse. You can shut him up for a fool … or you can fall at his feet and call him Lord and God. But let us not come with any patronising [sic] nonsense about His being a great human teacher. He has not left that open to us. He did not intend to.[11]

Jesus' claims do not leave us any other option except that He truly is both God and Man. Therefore, we have to make a choice to believe Him or walk away. Of course, the Bible confirms His claims and calls us to believe, because it is the perfect combination of these two that gives us hope. In fact, our salvation is counting on Jesus' claims to be true.

Jesus has to be God. Humanity, on its own, cannot save itself from sin. We are filthy with sin, and like the leopard, we cannot change our spots—our reward is death. Neither could the angels come to save us because they too are created. It had to be the Creator. The One who loves His creation so much that He would give up His own life for them—even if they hated Him. Furthermore, there's only One who could conquer death: the Author of Life; the Great I AM. Any other sacrifice is worthless, because it needed to be the Son of God on that tree. Jesus has to be God, and He is.

God's plan required more though. The Creator had to become one with His created—one *of* His created. In order to save us from our sins, He had to live the life we should have lived (in order to credit us with His righteousness) and die the death we should have died (in order to pay our debt to sin). He shared in our suffering so we would be able to share in His joy. He had to sweat, cry, laugh, walk, feel, hurt, bruise, and bleed. For it is by His stripes that we are healed. It is His blood that covers our sins. It is His death that redeems us. He had to take our place, because it needed to be the Son of Man on that tree. Jesus has to be man, and He is.

The Son of Man's hands were nailed to the cross;
The Son of God's love for you held Him there.
The Son of Man's body was broken by the cross;
The Son of God's heart was broken by your sin.
The Son of Man's blood was spilled for your sin;
The Son of God's blood was spilled for your redemption.
He is the Son of Man to understand you.
He is the Son of God to save you.

Yes, He is both God and man. This is why He loves us like He does. This is why He would die for us while we are still sinners. This is why He wants to help us succeed in our journey with Him. This is why the Gospel can proclaim: "For God so loved the world, that He gave His only Son, that whoever believes in him should not perish but have eternal life" (John 3:16).

What a blessing it is, that Jesus is the Son—the Son of God and the Son of Man!

•   •   •   •

Thank you, Father, for sending Your only Son, Jesus, to die for my sins. Thank you for loving me so much that You would give up so much to understand me. May I never forget the cost of my salvation.

---

[11] C.S. Lewis, *Mere Christianity* (New York: Simon & Schuster, 1996), 56.

"...I am the Lord, your healer."
– Exodus 15:26

13

The Healer

*I*n the days of the New Testament, there was a pool near the Sheep Gate in Jerusalem that was called Bethesda. This was no ordinary pool though. It was a pool that came with a legend. According to the stories, every so often an Angel of the Lord would come down to the pool and stir (some translations: "trouble") the waters. Then, whoever was the first into the pool after this stirring was healed. There must have been some evidence to the healing nature of this pool, otherwise there wouldn't have been so many waiting. For around this pool were five covered colonnades in which laid hundreds of people—all of whom suffered from some malady; all of whom were longing for the stirring of the waters.

It is into this scene that Jesus walked (John 5:1–6). I can only imagine what Jesus thought as He walked among so many who were sick and lame. So many opportunities for miracles. Of all the people there, His eyes fell upon a man who had been an invalid for 38 years. How long had he been waiting by the pool? Jesus knew it had been a long time, so He made that man His

103

mission. He waded through the multitude of people until He reached the man and then asked him a simple question: "Do you want to get well?"

What a strange question. Jesus was asking a man who had been sitting by a famous healing pool for 38 years. He hadn't been waiting for the water to warm up so he could take a leisurely dip in the pool and get a few laps in. This was a man who had been waiting patiently every day for the miraculous stirring of the waters just so he might somehow fall into the pool and gain the ability to walk out of it. "Do you want to get well?" Jesus asks. The man's answer speaks of lost hope: "Sir, I have no one to put me into the pool when the water is stirred up, and while I am going another steps down before me" (John 5:7).

The question seemed obvious. Do I want to get well? Yes, I want to get well, but I can't, I'm not fast enough. Do I want to get well? Of course I do, or I wouldn't be here. He had the desire, but his faith was wearing thin. A perfect situation for Jesus.

"Jesus said to him, 'Get up, take up your bed, and walk.' And at once the man was healed, and he took up his bed and walked" (John 5:8, 9). Here it is. The thing we all desire. The stories we like the best. "*At once* the man was healed." This is what we have become accustomed to expect when we hear the word "healed." This is what we long for when we think of healing: we want to be healed *at once*. Yet, we seem to forget that it isn't the method of healing that is important, but the Source of healing.

Before I go any further, though, I need to make something clear: *there is no true healing outside of Jesus, physical or otherwise.* He is the true source of healing. I say this because I find that too often we give man credit where credit is not due. Sure, mankind may accidentally stumble onto a cure for symptoms, but if we do it is only because God has allowed us to stumble upon information from His medical books. There is not a single dose of medical knowledge that hasn't come from our Creator.

Another reason I say this is because we can find physical healing from this collection of scientific knowledge, but still remain unwell. Likewise, we can find temporary spiritual help through various inspired writers, but continue to lack spiritual wellness. Only when Jesus is part of the equation will we find true healing. Jesus *is* the Way. Only He can make us well. For any kind of healing we need Jesus. Plain and simple.

Having established this foundation, we will examine some of the different types of healing we might experience—so we will become better at recognizing God as our healer and remember to praise Him.

One type of healing we have already seen, which is the type people desire and the easiest to recognize, is immediate healing. I mention it first only because it is the more popular one—the one more obvious to us. Jesus told the invalid to get up, and "at once" the man was healed. It was plain to see that Jesus healed him. Due to the nature of this type of healing, it is easier to recognize it as coming from God. Now, it isn't wrong to hope for immediate healing, because God still heals immediately in some cases. This *is* one of the ways God heals. Sometimes, in His great wisdom, God frees someone immediately. If God heals you immediately, do not forget to praise Him.

While this type of healing may be easier to recognize as from God, it is sad that, as we look to the other remaining types, their source becomes less and less obvious—to us, at least. As a result God receives less and less praise for them. Yet, it is still God who heals. Therefore, we need to look more carefully at those other ways of healing.

The next type of healing is gradual healing. A great example of this type is found in the story of the Ten Lepers recorded in Luke (Luke 17:11–14). Jesus was entering a village on His way to Jerusalem when ten lepers met Him at a distance. They yelled out, "Jesus, Master, have mercy on us." Jesus had pity on them and told them to go and show themselves to the Priest (this was required by someone who had been cured/cleaned from leprosy in order to enter back into the community). And as they went, they were healed.

They were not healed instantly. The healing came "as they went." It is noteworthy that only one of the lepers knew that God had healed him (Luke 17:15). I wonder: if Jesus had healed them immediately, would all ten have thanked Jesus for their healing? The reality, however, was that ninety percent didn't seem to recognize Him as the healer after their gradual healing. Maybe they thought the nice brisk walk back to the synagogue did them good. Maybe they were so excited that they just forgot to give God the credit. Whatever the reason, we have an example that though God doesn't always heal *immediately*, He does heal. So, it doesn't matter how long it takes—even if your healing is gradual—God should still be praised!

Another type of healing we find in the Bible is third-party healing. This would be a healing that takes place through a human source: physicians, nurses, and other medical personnel—sometimes through Prophets with anointing. (Remember, this is a type, not a way; Jesus is still the Way.) God will sometimes heal us through the medical knowledge or other natural methods He's revealed to us. An example of this is found in the story of Naaman (see 2 Kings 5:1–14). Long story short, Naaman had contracted leprosy and went to Israel to see a Prophet of God (as suggested by his servant girl). Elisha heard of the issue and sent a messenger to tell Naaman to dip in the Jordan River seven times and he would be healed. Naaman was expecting something more spectacular (and cleaner) and became angry. However, he was convinced by his servants to follow Elisha's instructions. After he did exactly as Elisha had said, he was healed.

God may heal us through medicines and other therapies even if we are hoping for a bigger bang. But when Naaman did what was required, he was healed. Did the water heal him? No. Did Elisha heal him? No. *God* healed him. Another example of such a healing is when Isaiah tells Hezekiah, "Let them take a cake of figs and apply it to the boil, that he may recover" (Isaiah 38:21). Isaiah gave the remedy, but it was still God who healed— He just did it through a human source. Who, then, deserves the praise? God does!

Another type of healing is healing at the Second Coming. This one isn't always accepted as a type of healing, because it is futuristic, but Paul described it well:

> Behold! I tell you a mystery. We shall not all sleep, but we shall all be changed, in a moment, in the twinkling of an eye, at the last trumpet. For the trumpet shall sound, and the dead will be raised imperishable, and we shall be changed. For this perishable body must put on the imperishable, and this mortal body must put on immortality. When the perishable puts on the imperishable, and the mortal puts on immortality, then shall come to pass the saying that is written: "Death is swallowed up in victory." "O death, where is your victory? O death, where is your sting?" (1 Corinthians 15:51–55)

He explained that while we have mortal, perishable lives now, that will all change at the last trumpet. He is saying, "You may be blind now, but *your* eyes will see Jesus' face. You may be deaf today, but *your* ears will hear Jesus calling your name. You may be physically impaired at this moment, but you will walk the streets of gold!" Why would Paul tell us this if not to let us know that no matter what we might be inflicted with during our lifetime, we will be completely healed at Jesus' coming?

Some may argue that there isn't any proof of this type of healing. Of course there isn't, because Jesus hasn't come yet! But just because we haven't experienced this healing yet does not mean we can't already praise God *in faith* for the healing we will receive! Take note of the words of Job in the midst of his suffering: "For I know that my Redeemer lives, and at the last he will stand upon the earth. And after my skin has been thus destroyed, yet in my flesh I shall see God" (Job 19:25, 26). It was his understanding that God did not have to heal him at that moment because he would be healed completely at Christ's coming. It was a hope that he looked forward to. This is a type of healing—new bodies and new lives at Christ's return. This is definitely another great reason to praise God!

Now, the final type, one we cannot forget: soul healing. In Psalm 147:3 David says, "He heals the brokenhearted and binds up their wounds." This healing goes much deeper than mere physical ailments. This is the type of healing the thief on the cross must have experienced when Jesus told him he would be in the kingdom. It is as these lyrics say, "sometimes He calms the storm, and other times He calms the child."[12] Sometimes, God needs to heal the soul. This one often goes with one of the other types. As a matter of fact, I believe that God uses this one more often than we think, if not every time. This is why there are so many promises in the Bible regarding the healing and restoring of souls. He can also heal emotional and spiritual pains and illnesses. Remember, Jesus cast out demons—not a physical impairment, but a spiritual one. He comforted those who were sad, or depressed, or fearful. He gave hope to those who thought they were doomed. He brought peace and joy to those suffering. If God has brought you emotional or spiritual healing, then praise Him! Because sometimes God heals the soul.

We are shown these different types of healing in order to remind us that Jesus still heals, and that He still wants to make us well. He may heal you immediately, in a grand miracle, or He may heal you gradually over time. He may heal you through the knowledge He has given medical personnel. He may wait and give you complete healing at His Second Coming. He'll even heal your heart and soul. But He will heal you!

We may never understand why God heals in different ways. Still, even though we may not be able to figure out when God will use a certain type of healing (I'm not sure it's our place to try to figure it out), we can be assured that He will heal. I am not trying to suggest that if you are deserving enough, God will use one type of healing, or if you have plenty of faith, He will use another type of healing. Nor am I trying to offer an explanation of why there is suffering or why some people are healed physically and some are not. What I am saying is that there is One who heals, and *only* One who heals—and in every healing, we need to recognize Him and praise Him!

This is the key: you don't need to remember any of the types of healing; just remember the Source of healing. God reminds us in Exodus 15:26, "I am the Lord, your healer." You see, God is not only the source of healing, but He wants you to know Him as *your* Healer. I'm sure you have experienced some kind of healing in your lifetime. So, if you have been given security, praise the Good Shepherd. If you have felt peace, praise the Refuge and Strength. If you have experienced forgiveness, praise the Savior. If you have received healing, praise the Great Physician. If you have been made well, praise Jesus!

"To the King of the ages, immortal, invisible, the only God, be honor and glory forever and ever. Amen" (1 Timothy 1:17).

• • • •

Father, forgive me for when I have failed to praise You. Forgive me for taking Your healing for granted. May Your praise be ever in my heart and on my lips, even in the midst of my pain.

---

[12] "Sometime He Calms the Storm," sung by Scott Krippayne, from the album *Wild Imagination*, Word Entertainment LLC, 1995.

"But when the goodness and loving kindness of God our Savior appeared, he saved us, not because of the works done by us in righteousness, but according to his own mercy…"
– Titus 3:4, 5

14

The Savior

There's no question that Jesus' life left a huge impact on humanity. He is one of the most debated persons in history. When He walked this earth, He brought peace and joy to almost all He encountered. Granted, there were some groups of theological thinkers who considered Him a rebel. He constantly challenged the popular religious thinking of the day. He overturned false theologies and brought people back to God's word. Basically, for those who had any religious influence, Jesus was a threat.

The leadership intended to end His influence, but instead they only increased it. Little did they know, but the solution they came up with to end the threat Jesus posed would quickly become one of the greatest reminders of God's love. It would become a symbol that would draw more people back to God than anything else since the dawn of man. Jesus said of His mission, "And I, when I am lifted up from the earth, will draw all men to myself" (John 12:32).

The Bible prophesied that Jesus would save us, but it would not be easy. Isaiah revealed the cost of our redemption:

> Surely he has borne our griefs and carried our sorrows; yet we esteemed him stricken, smitten by God, and afflicted. But he was pierced for our transgressions; he was crushed for our iniquities; upon him was the chastisement that brought us peace, and with his wounds we are healed. All we like sheep have gone astray; we have turned—every one—to his own way; and the Lord has laid on him the iniquity of us all. (Isaiah 53:4–6)

He would be pierced, crushed, and wounded. Yet, somehow these days, the cost of our salvation has been softened and romanticized. We have forgotten the true price Jesus paid. We have somehow diluted the "Savior" part of Jesus' ministry—the very thing that draws us to love Him in the first place. Thus, we need to be reminded.[13]

You see, in their desperation, the leaders of Israel did not think through what they were planning. Granted, it is quite difficult to think straight when you're furious. Only one thing mattered to them: they wanted to stop Jesus. They tried to embarrass Him, harass Him, and even arrest Him, but nothing seemed to work. After Jesus raised Lazarus from the dead, which caused many more to believe in Him, they began to realize that if they let Him continue like this, soon the whole world would believe. Therefore, they came to the conclusion that their only option to truly remove Jesus' influence was to remove Jesus (John 11:47–53)—even if it meant torturing and killing Him. By this time, they no longer cared. They just wanted Him gone.

They waited patiently for their opportunity and when it came, they pounced. Using one of Jesus' own disciples, they learned where Jesus would be (in the Garden of Gethsemane) and sent soldiers to arrest Him. But, to their (and the disciples') surprise, Jesus didn't resist. He allowed Himself to be taken and brought before the judicial system of the Jewish people, the Sanhedrin. From this point on, there was no way out—He was going to die.

Sadly, Jesus had no chance of a fair trial. First of all, according to the laws of the Sanhedrin,[14] they were not supposed to hold court from the evening sacrifices until after the morning sacrifices—since fair decisions were not as likely during those times. They were also not to meet on Festival days or the evening of Festivals. Yet, when was Jesus taken before them? On the Evening of Passover, long after the evening sacrifices. Furthermore, the Sanhedrin was to be a neutral party—listening to the accuser and the witnesses—yet, at Jesus' trial, *they* were the accusers. Do not miss this: Jesus had *no defense* in His trial. In addition, a conviction could only occur if they had two or three witnesses that observed the exact same thing. However, according the Bible, they couldn't get two people to even agree on what Jesus was being accused of! The best they could do was to gather three people who all mentioned Jesus saying the same thing (which, not surprisingly, was also taken out of context). Yet, the witnesses accusations were not enough for a death sentence (which they desired—John 18:31), so they were forced to move Him from the church's courts and bring Him to the Roman courts with a made-up charge of treason.

However, Pilate wanted nothing to do with the trial (possibly because of his wife's warning—Matthew 27:19) and tried passing Jesus off on Herod. Herod only wanted to see magic tricks, and when Jesus wouldn't comply, he had Jesus humiliated and sent Him back to Pilate. While Pilate tried several times to set Jesus free, the leaders wouldn't allow it. Jesus' punishment was even their suggestion. Crucifixion wasn't suggested by the Roman official, but by the leaders of Israel; it was recommended, not by a pagan nation but by God's own people. You can almost imagine the sound of the crowd, hatred building in their hearts, as their chanting grew louder and angrier: "*Crucify* Him!"

In one last attempt to release Jesus, Pilate called to the crowd, "Shall I crucify your King?" To which they replied, "We have no king but Caesar." Wow. One would expect that the *people of God* might have replied that *God* was their only King. Nope. Not during this moment of fury. God wasn't even on their minds.

During His time in the public judicial system, Jesus was mocked, spit on, and punched; He had His beard pulled out, had a crown made of thorns jammed on His head, and was brutally flogged.

"*He was oppressed and afflicted, yet He opened not His mouth*" (Isaiah 53:7).

The severity of the flogging would have left Jesus incredibly weak. The Roman flogging included pieces of bone or metal or wood attached onto one of several leather strands. These pieces were designed to dig into and rip out flesh—many times cutting so deep it would even expose the bones below. His back and sides would have been shredded and disfigured, with heavy blood loss.

"*…with His wounds we are healed.*"

It was in this state of pain and weakness that Jesus was made to bear the cross. The heavy beams of wood would have been placed on, and possibly strapped to, His shoulders. He was then forced to carry it through the streets of Jerusalem, paraded by the gathered crowd as a spectacle, out through the gates, and up to the hill where the crucifixion would take place. All the while, the people of the city watched, threw things at Him, and mocked Him. Imagine as Jesus walked down this path and looked to the faces in the crowd—some of who may have even been among the crowds who followed Him just weeks ago—which were now twisted with anger and hatred, or downcast in shame.

The pain became too great for Him to bear, though, and He collapsed under the weight of the cross before getting to the hill. Not wanting Jesus to die early, the Roman guards grabbed a man from the crowd to carry it the rest of the way (what a life-changing event that must have been).

At the hill, called Golgotha, they prepared Jesus for the cross. In a further effort to humiliate criminals, the Romans regularly crucified them naked. Therefore, Jesus would have been stripped of His clothes, His last bit of dignity, before they laid Him on the cross. Then, while one soldier held Him down, another soldier pounded the nails into His hands and feet. They didn't use nails like we have today—they weren't sharpened to a point—they used nails that would have been more like railroad spikes. Each time the hammer hit, it would send even more agonizing pain through His body.

"He was pierced for our transgressions."

Once His hands and feet were securely nailed, they raised the cross in the air and dropped it violently into a hole that would hold it in place—the nails tearing at His hands and feet. Crucifixion was designed in such a way that the feet were nailed so that the knees were bent. This caused all of His weight to be either on His hands or feet. When resting His weight on His hands, His arms would be raised above His head, making it difficult to breathe. In order to get a good breath and get relief from the pain in His hands, He would have had to push up with His legs, forcing all of His weight onto the nails holding His feet. It would have been more pain than you or I could even imagine. Yet, even in this pain He could still look at the crowd and say, "Father, *forgive them*, for they know not what they do" (Luke 23:34, emphasis mine). Remember: He endured all of that, not because of sins He had committed, but because of our sins. He had to be there for us to have any hope, so He accepted our hatred, our anger, and our rejection.

Sadly, His suffering didn't end there. Of all the pain that had come before, nothing would compare to the feeling He had that would cause Him to cry out, "My God, my God, why have you forsaken [forgotten] me?" (Mark 15:34). Have you ever felt like God has forgotten about you? If so, then you might have a slight idea of what Jesus was going through. Except, our typical reaction is to become angry with God if we feel He has forgotten us, whereas Jesus felt anguish from losing someone immensely adored by Him. All through His life, Jesus enjoyed a very close relationship to His Father in Heaven. Yet, at this moment of great misery, He could not feel the Father's presence. As He hung on that cross, He felt abandoned.

What happened? God promises never to leave or forsake us, so He didn't leave. The Bible tells us that our sins separate us from God. I believe it was at this moment that our sins were placed on Christ. "*And the Lord has laid on Him the iniquity of us all*" (Isaiah 53:6). As it says in 1 Peter 2:24, "He himself bore our sins in his body on the tree, that we might die to sin and live to righteousness. By his wounds you have been healed."

Yet, it was more than this. Jesus didn't just carry our sins. Galatians 3:13 says, "Christ redeemed us from the curse of the law by becoming a curse for us." Notice how Paul described it in 2 Corinthians 5:21. "For our sake he made him to be sin who knew no sin, so that in him we might become the righteousness of God." Friend, Jesus didn't just take our sins. He *became* sin. And the result of Him becoming sin for us was separation from His Father—something far worse than all the torture man could ever place upon Him.

Not long after this, Jesus said, "It is finished." "Father, into your hands I commit my spirit" (John 19:30; Luke 23:46), and breathed His last breath. He died hated and tortured by man, and separated from God. "But God shows his love for us in that while we were still sinners, Christ died for us" (Romans 5:8).

You see, friend, the nails did not hold Jesus on the cross; His love for you did. Any time that day, Jesus could have said, "enough!" And angels would have come to His rescue. But He didn't. He stayed on the cross. He accepted the cross. Galatians 1:4 says that Jesus *gave* Himself to us in order to rescue us from sin. That means He *willingly* went through this for you. He willing became sin for you. So when He died on the cross, sin died on the cross—the penalty that your sins had required was *fully paid* (Romans 8:3, 4; 1 Peter 1:18–20). Praise the Lord!

He did not stay on the cross because we deserved it either. As Paul writes,

> But when the goodness and loving kindness of God our Savior appeared, he saved us, not because of the works done by us in righteousness, but according to his own mercy, by the washing of regeneration and renewal of the Holy Spirit, whom he poured out on us richly through Jesus Christ our Savior, so that being justified by his grace we might become heirs according to the hope of eternal life. (Titus 3:4–7)

He remained on the cross because of His own mercy. He endured all of that pain and suffering because He loves you. *You were the reason He stayed on the cross.* Because His death makes it possible for you to have eternal life; it makes it possible for you to be forgiven.

How can we forget such a wonderful Savior? How can we forget the incredible cost of our salvation? We do this anytime we refuse to accept His offer of salvation and attempt to create our own. Here's the thing to remember: "the wages of sin is death" (Romans 6:23), and "without the shedding of blood there is no forgiveness" (Hebrews 9:22). So, death is required in the payment of sin. One way or another, your sins will be paid for—either through Christ's sacrifice on your behalf, or by you.

Won't you run to your Savior and accept His sacrifice right now? If you will, I encourage you to pray this prayer:

• • • •

Father, I am a sinner; I cannot save myself.
I want to accept Jesus' sacrifice on my behalf right now.
Please forgive me for my sins. Cleanse me from all my
unrighteousness. Keep me from trying to save myself.
Let me never forget the cost of my salvation.

---

13 The full story of Jesus' sacrifice is found in Matthew 26:47–27:60, Mark 14:43–15:46, Luke 22:47–23:53, and John 18:1–19:42.

14 For more information about the Sanhedrin, check out this webpage: http://www.thesanhedrin.org—especially their page on "The 'Sanhedrin' in the New Testament." Interestingly, modern Rabbinic Judaism rejects the idea that the Sanhedrin tried Jesus due to the fact that the Talmud does not record this trial. However, it would make sense that any trial that went against the normal rules of the judicial body would not be recorded.

"I am the resurrection and the life.
Whoever believes in me, though he die, yet shall he live."
– *John 11:25*

15

The Conqueror

*I*magine the greatest disappointment you have experienced and then increase it several times more. There have been other events in history that have been labeled disappointments, even a "Great Disappointment," but none could have come close to what the disciples must have experienced.

Try to put yourself in their situation. Leading up to Jesus' death on the cross, they became more and more convinced that He was the Messiah—He was the One who would save them. Yet, the impossible happened. Something more horrible than they could ever have imagined. Their Savior died.

It didn't matter how often Jesus tried to tell them He would die; it didn't matter how the prophesies said He would die. It was still something they were not expecting. They knew as we know that everyone eventually dies, but even though the loss of someone hurts, it is most painful when someone dies before we expected. In their minds, Jesus' ministry had just started. He had only been actively in ministry for three and a half years. On top of that, He was only recently getting the recognition and attention He deserved. People all over were starting to believe in Him. Only a few days before He died, when entering Jerusalem on a donkey, the crowd had welcomed Jesus as a king (John 12:12, 13). Now, suddenly, all of that was gone. Everything He had worked so hard for was over.

Understand that, at first, the cross was not a symbol of victory. To the disciples, the cross was a symbol of the end— the end of Jesus' life, the end of their ministries, and the end of their hopes. They could not see past the cross. Witnessing their Teacher, Savior, and best friend hanging on the cross had to be devastating. Sure, Jesus had healed the sick and even raised the dead, but how could He do that if *He* was dead? In their minds, all was lost.

In this moment of defeat, they forgot. Of course, in moments of great trials we all have a tendency to forget things. So when this dark cloud of grief consumed them, all He had taught before was pushed from their memories. If they had remembered, they would have been encouraging the people that Jesus would rise again—just as He had told them plenty of times before (see Luke 9:22, 18:31–33; Matthew 20:17–19). If they had remembered, they would have been preaching the power of the resurrection in the streets of Jerusalem that very day (they had not long before experienced that power with Lazarus—John 11:17–44). But they weren't encouraging or preaching. Instead, they were huddled in a secret room, afraid that they, His followers, would be next.

Their forgetfulness at this moment is understandable. Their whole world came crashing down; their entire belief system was demolished. They were not able to think clearly. That Friday afternoon they could only watch through tear-blurred vision as the religious leadership, with help from the Romans, murdered their God. The next day was supposed to be a High Sabbath (due to it being a Sabbath of Passover as well—John 19:31), but it would only be a day of great sorrow, confusion, and growing fear for those who believed in Christ. In their understanding, Jesus was gone, once and for all.

Some did remember Jesus' teachings, but not who you might expect. The Chief Priests and the Pharisees—those who pushed to kill Jesus—remembered Jesus saying that He would rise on the third day and they shared their concerns about it with Pilate. They suggested that the tomb should be secured so the disciples wouldn't come and steal the body and claim Jesus had risen. Pilate granted them a guard of soldiers and told them to make it as secure as they could (Matthew 27:62–65). Thus, it was not Rome, but the Priests and the Pharisees who secured the tomb and set the guard—they wanted to guarantee that they were finished with Jesus, once and for all.

However, very early on Sunday morning, something occurred that would bring more joy than anyone could have imagined. Whereas the cross would one day be a reminder for people of the abundant love of God, the tomb would remind mankind of the magnificent power of God. That morning, a few women made their way to the tomb. They needed to anoint Jesus' body with the traditional burial spices, since they did not do it the day before (Luke 23:56–24:1). Imagine them walking quietly towards to tomb together, tears in their eyes. They needed to do this, but it would only bring back all the pain from Friday.

No matter what they thought they would see when they arrived, they were not expecting what they actually saw: the stone was rolled away and the tomb was *empty*. We might expect that they would have celebrated, but they didn't rejoice or start a praise service. Luke 24:4 says that they were perplexed. They were at a loss as to what happened. In the original Greek, the word "perplexed" carries with it the implication of serious anxiety. Seeing the empty tomb didn't make them excited—it made them scared!

Of course, this makes sense. What would you expect if you went to visit a loved one's grave and found it empty? Would you celebrate that the person was now alive? I doubt it. I would expect that you'd be scared or angry, or both. Likewise, their first thoughts would not have been that Jesus was alive; their fears were most likely similar to what the leadership had held: someone had stolen Jesus' body.

While they were trying to figure out what happened, two men appeared by them in bright clothing. Of course, when you are already anxious about one thing, the unexpected appearance of another unexplainable thing can be terrifying, and it was (especially in a *cemetery*). But the two glowing men were angels coming to comfort them. They told the women that Jesus was not there because He had risen—just as He said He would.

Suddenly, things started to make sense (Luke 24:8). As they returned to the city, Jesus' words came back to their minds. They quickly went and told the disciples what had happened. As soon as they explained, the room broke out with praise and thanksgiving, right? Not exactly. The disciples thought it was nonsense—it couldn't be possible (Luke 24:11)! No matter how much they may have *wanted* it to be true, that kind of thing just didn't happen. Besides, they had all seen Him hanging on the cross and they had all seen Him die.

Something the women said must have triggered a spark in Peter and John. Was it just curiosity, or was it hope? Whatever it was, they couldn't resist and they ran to the tomb (John 20:3–8). They found it just as the women had described it: empty.

I'm not sure we could begin to understand what was going through their minds. A flood of emotions, no doubt. A glimmer of hope? A moment of fear? There they stood, inside an empty grave. Yet, the empty grave would not have registered automatically as a victory over death. It would be more plausible that someone stole the body to further humiliate their Master. But who would do something like this, and why? Adding to the confusion of the situation: the grave clothes were neatly folded (John 20:7). What grave robber would do that?

Then, the truly unimaginable happened: after returning to Jerusalem, Jesus appeared to them. Could they believe their eyes? Was this just a dream? Was it really Jesus standing in front of them? How? Yet, there was no doubt—it was definitely Him. Jesus had already appeared to Peter (Luke 24:34), Mary Magdalene (John 20:11–17), and the disciples on the road to Emmaus (Luke 24:13–31). He even made a special appearance later for Thomas, so he would believe as well (John 20:26–28). Tears of sorrow were replaced with tears of joy. If the cross revealed sacrifice and pain, the empty tomb revealed joy and victory. The cross took away their hope, and seeing Jesus again brought back that hope, a thousand times greater. If they had remembered, Jesus told them this would happen: "So also you have sorrow now, but I will see you again, and your hearts will rejoice, and no one will take your joy from you" (John 16:22).

Now the words of Jesus came back with great power: "I am the resurrection and the life. Whoever believes in me, though he die, yet shall he live" (John 11:25). Sure, they knew about the future resurrection—Martha spoke of it just before Jesus made that statement. They may have even known the prophecy in Isaiah 26:19, which notes, "Your dead shall live; their bodies shall rise. You who dwell in the dust, awake and sing for joy! For your dew is a dew of light, and the earth will give birth to the dead." They had already lived with the hope of the resurrection. But before Jesus, that's all it was: hope.

For most of us, hope is complicated thing. We often hope for things that never end up happening (especially when our hope is mistakenly placed in humanity). Students can graduate with a great degree from a great university with the hope of a great career, only to find themselves stuck in a dead-end job that they hate. Seekers of the truth can walk into a church with the hope of finding a place of healing and acceptance, only to find themselves judged and rejected. A disciple could follow Jesus with the hope that He was truly the Messiah, the chosen one of God, only to witness His death. So, while the resurrection was definitely a hope for the people of God, until seeing Jesus had risen from the dead, they hadn't *experienced* its truth. At that moment, the resurrection was no longer simply a hope for them—it was a reality. The One who had the power to raise the dead had now completely conquered death and the grave. That day, they had encountered His power first hand.

Jesus standing in front of them after such a grueling few days removed any doubt that He was the Son of God. It proved that absolutely nothing—not even death—was impossible for God to overcome. What's even greater is that this power of the resurrection would now also empower the people of God. As Paul said, "we were buried therefore with him by baptism into death, in order that, just as Christ was raised from the dead by the glory of the Father, we too might walk in the newness of life" (Romans 6:4). The power that raised Jesus from the dead is the same power that can live in our lives. That same power can make us victorious in our spiritual walk as well. It is that power that guarantees our hope for a renewed relationship with God.

Of course, Jesus rising from the dead was only the beginning. Notice what Paul wrote in 1 Corinthians 15:20: "But in fact, Christ has been raised from the dead, the firstfruits of those who have fallen asleep." The firstfruits are the sign of the beginning of the harvest. In other words, Jesus was the just the beginning of all who would be resurrected. And it gets more exciting as we read more: "For as by a man came death, by a man has come also the resurrection of the dead. For as in Adam all die, so also in Christ shall all be made alive" (1 Corinthians 15:21, 22). Jesus completely conquered death and the grave! No longer would death be able to hold anyone who trusts in Him.

This is another vital truth about Jesus of which we must be reminded. This should be the story that is constantly on our lips: Jesus is risen from the dead! Jesus holds the keys to death and the grave. Because of Jesus' resurrection, we have the *assurance* of seeing our loved ones again. Because of Jesus' victory, we can look forward to the reality of what Paul describes in 1 Thessalonians 4:14–18:

> For since we believe that Jesus died and rose again, even so, through Jesus, God will bring with him those who have fallen asleep. For this we declare to you by a word from the Lord, that we who are alive, who are left until the coming of the Lord, will not precede those who have fallen asleep. For the Lord himself will descend from heaven with a cry of command, with the voice of an archangel, and with the sound of the trumpet of God. And the dead in Christ will rise first. Then we who are alive, who are left, will be caught up together with them in the clouds to meet the Lord in the air, and so we will always be with the Lord. Therefore, encourage one another with these words.

Jesus is no longer dead! We serve a *risen* Savior. These should be encouraging words. There is not a shrine or memorial you can visit for a teacher named Jesus who passed away long ago. Sure, I know that you could see an empty tomb in Israel today that is *suggested* to be Jesus' tomb, but *any* empty tomb could be His (it's not as though Jesus carved into the walls "Jesus wuz here"). Why? Because He is *no longer dead*. Jesus is alive. This means death no longer has power over us. This means that someday we can see the loved ones we've lost to death. Jesus' victory over death and the grave means that eternal life is no longer simply a hope; rather, it is a reality for those who trust in Him. Power for spiritual victories in this life and life eternal can be ours because our Savior lives. As the beloved hymn declares, "Because He lives, I can face tomorrow. Because He lives all fear is gone. Because I know He holds the future, and life is worth the living just because He lives."

Do not forget: the One who desires this relationship with you is a *living* God. The very fact that you are able to get to know Jesus is because He is risen. And the power that raised Him from the grave is the same power that will give you new life today and make it possible for you to rise when Jesus comes.

• • • •

Father, thank you for reminding me of Your power and majesty. Thank you for conquering death and the grave so I can look forward to the resurrection and life eternal with You. I want to be among those who rise to meet you in the air.

"And if I go and prepare a place for you, I will come again and will take you to myself, that where I am you may be also."
– John 14:3

16

The Coming King

For forty days after His spectacular resurrection, Jesus appeared to the disciples and continued to teach them (Acts 1:3). He told them about the work of the kingdom they were to finish. He told them about the coming Holy Spirit and the power that would come upon them. Then, one day, right before their eyes, He suddenly rose up in the air, into the clouds, and disappeared from their sight (Acts 1:9).

The disciples stood there staring at the sky. We can understand why. That is not something you see everyday. Besides, they had just gotten Jesus back! They thought they had lost Him once. Did they just lose Him again? Then, while they were looking intently at the sky, two angels appeared. They assured them—reminded them—that He was coming back: "This Jesus, who was taken up from you into heaven, will come in the same way as you saw him go into heaven" (Acts 1:11). There won't

127

be a substitute Jesus, or a similar Jesus, but *this* Jesus—the same Jesus you grew to know; the same Jesus you fell in love with; the same Jesus you depend on—is coming back again.

The disciples joyfully returned to Jerusalem and soon began the powerful work of spreading the good news: Jesus Christ is risen from the dead, and He is coming again soon (simple message, but powerful). It was a message they preached with great passion and conviction.

Unfortunately, that passion and conviction of Jesus' return would lessen. According to Peter, in the last days scoffers will come and say, "Where is the promise of his coming? For ever since the fathers fell asleep, all things are continuing as they were from the beginning of creation" (2 Peter 3:4). Basically, they have heard that message so many times in so many ways for so long—and nothing seems different—that they question the truth of the message.

Perhaps you have come to feel this way as well. Maybe you can remember when you used to be excited about Jesus' coming, but so much time has passed and that excitement has passed as well. Sure, you know He's coming *sometime*, but it doesn't feel like it will be any time soon. We have come to a point in Christianity where we have heard that "Jesus is coming soon" so often that we don't really believe it—at least, we don't live like we believe it. Maybe we have forgotten why this truth about Jesus is so important. We need another reminder.

You see, Jesus warned the disciples the night He was arrested that He would have to leave them, but promised them He would return. We should revisit this promise:

> Let not your hearts be troubled. Believe in God; believe also in me. In my Father's house are many rooms. If it were not so, would I have told you that I go to prepare a place for you? And if I go and prepare a place for you,

I will come again and will take you to myself, that where
I am you may be also. (John 14:1–3)

Jesus told them He had to leave because He was going to
prepare a place for us. He promised that once that was finished,
He would return.

Maybe it is taking so long for Jesus to return because He
has a lot to do to prepare a place for us. I know some imagine
Jesus with a tool-belt and a hammer pounding nails into the
newly added walls inside our heavenly mansions, as if the
"preparations" for us were merely physical. Of course, if Jesus
left earth to simply build a few extra rooms for those going to
Heaven, why couldn't He just speak them into existence? He
has done it before! If that were all He had to do, He would have
been there and back in only moments. It would seem that the
preparations were greater than making a few extra rooms.
(Besides, His Father's house already has many rooms!)

First of all, we need to understand what "quickly" means to
God. Peter said that "with the Lord one day is as a thousand years,
and a thousand years as one day" (2 Peter 3:8). As I mentioned
in chapter 11, before we assume this is some kind of prophetic
key for time, we must recognize that Peter said one day is "*as*"
a thousand years, not one day "*is*" a thousand years. In case
there may still be some confusion, Psalm 90:4 further explains:
"For a thousand years in your sight are but as yesterday when it
is past, or as a watch in the night." Simply put: God does not
view time as we do. What can seem like forever to beings
whose life span averages less than 100 years will seem like just a
moment to a Being who lives forever. Therefore, "quickly" for
God, may not be "quickly" for us. Plus, Jesus told us that no one
knows the day or the hour of His return except for the Father
(Matthew 24:36), and if you don't know exactly when, He may
seem late even when He's on time.

So why does it seem like He's taking forever? According to Peter, "The Lord is not slow to fulfill his promise as some count slowness, but is patient toward you, not wishing that any should perish, but that all should reach repentance" (2 Peter 3:9). If He seems to be taking forever, it is because He is patient. He's not trying to rush salvation. He wants to save as many as possible. Praise the Lord!

You see, Jesus had a much greater work in mind when He left to "prepare a place for us." The cross was not the end of the Plan of Salvation; it was just the beginning—it was the payment. The payment still had to be applied. While Jesus' ministry on earth was finished, He had one more work of ministry to fulfill. We find it described in the book of Hebrews:

> But when Christ appeared as a high priest of the good things that have come, then through the greater and more perfect tent (not made with hands, that is, not of this creation) he entered once for all into the holy places, not by means of the blood of goats and calves but by means of his own blood, thus securing an eternal redemption. (Hebrews 9:11, 12)

This passage describes a different aspect of Jesus' ministry— that of High Priest. It is not an aspect of His ministry often taught. Yet, it is an extremely important one since it is through this ministry that Jesus *secures* for us our eternal redemption. So where does this phase of His ministry occur? The author of Hebrews says that Jesus enters into "the holy places." Reading further down in the chapter explains what this means.

> For Christ has entered, not into holy places made with hands, which are copies of the true things, but *into heaven itself*, now to appear in the presence of God on

our behalf. Nor was it to offer himself repeatedly, as the high priest enters the holy places every year with blood not his own, for then he would have had to suffer repeatedly since the foundation of the world. But as it is, he has appeared once for all at the end of the ages to put away sin by the sacrifice of himself. (Hebrews 9:24–26, emphasis mine)[15]

After His resurrection and ascension, when Jesus entered into heaven, He entered into the Holy and Most Holy Places of heaven as our High Priest. This is a very interesting description of Jesus' heavenly work.

The only reason a High Priest went into the Most Holy Place was for the yearly Day of Atonement Festival. It was the only time, and only reason, *anyone* entered into the Most Holy Place. To the people of Israel, it was the day the sanctuary would be cleansed of their sins. In other words, when that day was over, those who had trusted in God and the sacrifice for their sins were at peace with God—cleansed completely from all their sins (Leviticus 16:30). It is the concept behind 1 John 1:9, "If we confess our sins, he is faithful and just to forgive us our sins and to cleanse us from all unrighteousness." It was also seen as a day of judgment for them—whatever sins were not confessed and cleansed from the sanctuary on that solemn day were then the responsibility of the person who committed them (and they remained guilty of their sins).

Why is this important? Paul tells us in 2 Corinthians 5:10, "For we must all appear before the judgment seat of Christ, so that each one may receive what is due for what he has done in the body, whether good or evil." We will all face judgment someday. Some believe this means that we will all have to stand physically before God in some heavenly courtroom—typically occurring immediately after we die. However, the Bible says that Jesus is "the one appointed by God to be judge of the living and the dead" (Acts 10:42; see also 2 Timothy 4:1). Furthermore, Acts 17:31 says that God has "fixed," or selected, a day to judge the world through Jesus. Thus, judgment will occur at a specific time and will concern *both* those living and those dead (so it couldn't only be after we die).

In addition, Jesus said that when He returns, He will reward everyone according to their works (Matthew 16:27, see also Revelation 22:12). According to what we just read we must appear before the judgment seat of Jesus so that we can receive our reward, yet Jesus is coming with His reward.

How can this happen? Remember what we read in Revelation 14:7—"Fear God and give him glory, because the hour of his judgment has come." This is a message that will go out into the world in the last days. Therefore, the judgment of the dead and the living will take place *before* Jesus returns.

This means, when Jesus returns, *our judgment has already been decided*—whether or not we have accepted His sacrifice on our behalf—and our reward for our decision is coming with Him. This is why we cannot wait to make our decision for Christ. When we see Jesus coming in the clouds it will be too late to pick a side. Some may suggest that you wait until we get closer to His coming, or until you've experienced more of the world, but what if something happens to you while you are waiting to make your decision? What if, God forbid, you do not make it to tomorrow? *Today* is the day to choose! Please understand that postponing your choice for Christ *is* making a choice.

Reading further in the passage in Hebrews 9, we see what the reward is: "And just as it is appointed for man to die once, and after that comes judgment, so Christ, having been offered once to bear the sins of many, will appear a second time, not to deal with sin but to save those who are eagerly waiting for him" (verses 27 and 28). When Jesus comes, there is no more work to be done toward eradicating sin. It is finished (see John 19:30 and Revelation 16:17). He will not be coming to die again and He will not be coming to try to fix the world; He will be coming as King of kings and Lord of lords to bring salvation to those who are waiting for Him (Revelation 19:11–16).

This means we must continue to wait—patiently. It may seem like Jesus is taking a long time to come, but He *is* coming soon! We can know He is coming soon because He said so. Just in the last chapter of the Bible, Jesus says three times, "I am coming soon" (Revelation 22:7, 12, 20). Why do you say something three times? For emphasis and to help people remember. In other words, Jesus *is* coming soon!

And what a glorious day that will be! He will come "in the clouds with great power and glory" (Mark 13:26). Loved ones will be reunited. Those who have died holding on to Christ will rise and all the righteous will rise to meet Jesus in the air to live with Him forever (1 Thessalonians 4:16, 17). We will be raised with, or transformed into, brand new immortal, glorious bodies (1 Corinthians 15:51–53). Those who have waited on the Lord will receive their reward: eternal life with Him.

Still, we do not know the day or the hour, so we wait. That day will come upon the world like a thief, so we wait. Of course, waiting does not mean sitting in a church pew doing nothing. While we wait, we finish the work of sharing the Gospel—sharing your experience of the love of God with others. While we wait, we encourage each other to stay on the journey. And as Peter said, "since you are waiting for these, be diligent to be found [in] him without spot or blemish, and at peace" (2 Peter 3:14). While we wait, we should be strengthening and deepening our relationship with Christ so we'll know Him when He comes.

Friend, I'm sure you have heard this before. I know it may have become just another saying to you, but Jesus *is* coming soon. Sometimes it feels like He is taking forever. Other times, you may think that He should take His time. Jesus may come in our lifetime and He may not. He may come a hundred years from now or He may come this year, but *He will come.* Regardless, you do not want to wait to see what might develop in the prophetic signs before making your decision for Him. Choose today, right now. You are not guaranteed tomorrow. When your life on earth is done, your decision will have been made. Were you holding on to Jesus, or were you holding on to something else? Yes, one day—a day already set by the Father—Jesus will come, whether you are ready or not.

It is my prayer that you have found a strengthened and renewed relationship with Jesus. If you have, do not let go. Be patient and wait on Him. If you are still on the fence of decision, I encourage you review again the character of the God who wants to be your friend. He is trustworthy and faithful, He loves you, and He can save you. Regardless of how slow His timing may appear, God is patiently trying to save as many as possible. He may be waiting for *you.*

Yes, friend, *this* Jesus—the same Jesus we have learned about in this book—*your* Jesus, is coming soon with salvation for you! Hold on to Him, and one day you will be among those who declare, "Behold, this is our God; we have waited for Him, that he might save us. This is the Lord; we have waited for him; let us be glad and rejoice in his salvation" (Isaiah 25:9).

• • • •

Father, I want to be ready when Jesus comes. Give me the patience to wait. Give me the strength to hold on even when it seems to be taking so long. Give me the courage and passion to spread the good news of Jesus' coming to those around me.

---

[15] This is speaking of the same place that is described as God's "temple in heaven" in Revelation 11:19.

"Those who are victorious
will inherit all this,
and I will be their God
and they will be my children."
Revelation 21:7 (NIV)

For further studies on this and other topics, visit the author's blog at:
www.overcominglaodicea.org

Also available by Bill Kasper:

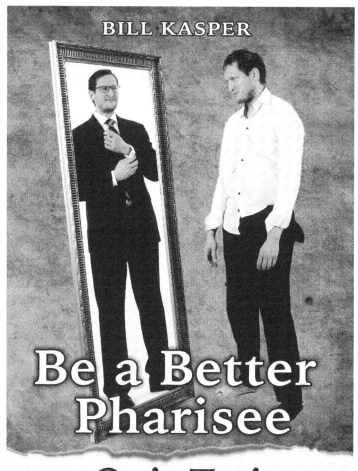

or Quit Trying

45213782R00085

Made in the USA
San Bernardino, CA
03 February 2017